THE BLACKBELT
MASTERMIND

ISBN-13: 978-0992892401

Illustrations © Danielle Serpico
Edited by Rachel Moore

2014
By
The BlackBelt MasterMind ™
M.A.S.T.E.R. ™ System

Printed
by Create Space

THE BLACKBELT MASTERMIND

The Ultimate Guide to
Having a Fighter Mindset and Winning in Life

Danielle Serpico

The M.A.S.T.E.R™ System

Masterful attitude,
strength and tenacity equal results...

For Alan.
You are both my Yin and my Yang.
My light and my shade.
Not only my greatest love but also my greatest teacher.
This book would not have been possible
without your superb mind.

Thank you

To the woman
whom as a petulant teenager,
I once said, I did not want to grow up to be like -
I now also,
search for my glasses upon my head,
write and draw all day without pausing for breath
and sing with crazy abandon to anything Latino.
My creativity is your creation
for I have now become you, with pride.

I am my mother's daughter.

This book is for you

CONTENTS

ACKNOWLEDGEMENTS – PAGE 6

LETTER OF INFLUENCE BY MARINA NANI - PAGE 7

FOREWORD BY RAYMOND AARON - PAGE 9

BEFORE THIS BOOK – PAGE 11

INTRODUCING YOU TO THE MASTER SYSTEM – PAGE 14

CHAPTER ONE – BEGINNING WITH THE WHITE BELT - PAGE 24

CHAPTER TWO – YELLOW & MASTERFUL AWARENESS – PAGE 35

CHATER THREE – ORANGE ATTITUDE – PAGE 51

CHAPTER FOUR – PURPLE STRENGHT - PAGE 72

CHAPTER FIVE – BLUE TENACITY - PAGE 88

CHAPTER SIX – GREEN EQUALS BALANCE – PAGE 105

CHAPTER SEVEN – BROWN RESULTS – PAGE 120

CHAPTER EIGHT – CONCLUDING WITH THE BLACK BELT – PAGE 140

RESOURCES & FURTHER READING –PAGE 144

ABOUT THE AUTHOR – PAGE 145

ACKNOWLEDGEMENTS

This book is for me, the joining of the dots. Finally, the lines are beginning to become clear. The dots in this case are the many people whom I have had the honour and privilege of meeting, knowing or training with.

I am extremely grateful for all my learnings in Neuro-Linguistic Programming, co - created by Richard Bandler and John Grinder.
I have had the greatest fortune and honour to train directly with Richard Bandler. His work has most definitely helped 'make my life great' and by no means a small thing, it gave me the courage to paint again after nearly 20 years.
A huge thank you to John La Valle and Kathleen La Valle and The Society of NLP who's training, talented skills and humour have been invaluable.

I would also like to extend my gratitude and thanks to
Owen Fitzpatrick, the Charisma expert in real life and on the stage.
To Paul McKenna for his inspirational techniques and great mastery.
To Justin Tranz for teaching me to Dare 2 Fail.
To all the other huge talents I have been fortunate enough to train and learn from.

To Raymond Aaron for his great wisdom and teachings,
without which this book would never have become more
than simply a seed of a thought in my mind.
To Marina Nani, the truest of roses amongst roses,
your momentum and your passion is most definitely inspirational.
Thank you for coming into my life and sharing your heart with me.

To all I have trained with in Martial Arts especially Tommy Jordan whose dedication to his art and pragmatism in its execution is the mark of a true Black Belt. To Erle Montaigue whose knowledge and integrity in his art was only surpassed by his genuine warmth and kindness, thank you '*Beautiful*'.
To my teacher and Sensei, Alan Ellis for his complete integrity, passion and dedication in passing on all of his boundless knowledge of the Martial Arts, both to me and all of his students.
Thank you for teaching me how to get back up.

Finally, thank you to all my true friends who have supported me,
my clients and anyone who has opened up their lives to me
and shared with me the intimacy of their problems and issues.
Your courage, strength and watching your transformations
is what keeps this passion alive.

LETTER OF INFLUENCE BY MARINA NANI

Imagine this gigantic, heavy, bolted door, which I had looked at for decades. I could never imagine what was behind it or the journey that would start, once I was on the other side. If you are reading this book, you are now at the beginning of the most extraordinary journey - The Journey from Intellectual to Experimental, and your heart's desire is guiding you in the right direction.

Danielle Serpico - and Danielle Serpico alone - made me understand the reason I felt disconnected from myself for decades, and that sole discovery walked me out of my own fog. Now, I have a clear vision and all seems too easy, when going through the many decisions I face daily.

There are some things that changed dramatically in my life since Danielle walked in: I discovered the power of words. I think better using the right words, and because I think clearly, I make better decisions. I learned to use language with greater precision and elegance, so that communication flows and the message I have in my mind stays fresh and crisp all the way to my audience. Learning how to motivate myself helps me motivate others.

As an immediate result, I no longer feel overwhelmed from the past hurdles which had prevented me from taking my business to the next level. I truly feel that I achieved that competitive advantage and increased my profits, all thanks to Danielle's power of masterminding.

If I felt bewildered before, if I was resisting my mission in life, now I am ready to be who I am meant to be!

Danielle can show you that you are ready to make the difference in your own life and for those you love, because you are the only one who can. She will help you identify and hover through your existing limitations that are holding you back in your life right NOW. Her program will work out the few miracles you need and one thing is for sure: you will learn how to bribe the 'Gate Keeper' of your mind, the one who made you feel unfit for the change you need, the change that can only start within.

By mastering your subconscious mind, you will fast track your wildest dreams simply because what Danielle Serpico is teaching is the 'why' and the 'what' that will make your conscious mind (your Gate Keeper) embrace the change you are craving for.

If there was ever a black belt for winning the fight with your own demons and achieving victory over yourself, then you are in the right place, for you are very soon to become the champion of your own life.

Marina Nani,
Author, Public Speaker, Entrepreneur
www.marinanani.com

Foreword by
RAYMOND AARON
New York Times Bestselling Author

The training of a fighter is well-known as a meticulous disciplined enterprise. True grit and hard knocks are the order of the day. You're on the canvas of life. Your muddied, semiconscious, incoherent brain is listening to the referee's 10-count.

It is at this point when even courage and tenacity fail, when intestinal fortitude abandons you, that you need the one thing that every great champion who has ever stepped into the ring of life possesses - a mentor, a confidant, a coach, an angel on your shoulder.

In your hand you are holding a book that contains the wisdom of such a motivational figure. Danielle Serpico has earned her stripes in the jungle of life; battling through personal, emotional and financial adversity to emerge a true champion. Her experiences chronicle her pathway to success.

In this book you will find the strategies that she used to develop her acclaimed M.A.S.T.E.R.™ System. From an entrepreneurial businesswoman and European martial arts champion to a Master NLP trainer and coach, Danielle has evolved her system with one goal in mind – your success.

This book contains all the practical exercises and easily assimilated techniques you need in order to develop your inner warrior. Utilizing the key principles of her system, you will learn to become the master of your mind and ultimately master of your destiny.

Whether battling for victory in your personal life or in your business, the M.A.S.T.E.R.™ system is an easy-to-follow step-by-step personal coaching method that works. Using cutting edge NLP technology, sports & self-defence psychology and a life time of experience, this book builds a comprehensive matrix of success strategies.

'Masterful attitude, strength and tenacity equal results', is the key basis of her system. Danielle is always in your corner, watching your back, as you engage in your most rewarding endeavour yet, the creation of a wonderful and rewarding life.

Before this book...

They watched in silence, not knowing what to say or do. I sat, slumped in a patch of glittering dust particles, as the sun shone a spotlight on me. On the 5th of June 2009, after 17 years in business I had just closed the doors to the last of my three beloved restaurants.

'Now what?' I thought, 'What am I supposed to do now?'

I did what any true fighter knows to do.

I got back up and gave life my best shot.

What happened over the next five years was to prove the most transformational journey yet. I immersed myself in the mind and its workings. I studied hard and listened to the best experts in their field. I met the most incredible people in this time and made many lifelong friends. Most of all I discovered the real me; the fighter that lies beneath my nearly always smiling face.

I became aware of my internal chatter and the critical sabotaging part of me that sometimes terrorised my mind. I learned how to silence it and how to replace it with a more positive and productive voice.

I let go of many useless fears and started to re-embrace life fully with gusto. I painted for the first time in nearly twenty years and actually loved my own work. I was proud of myself and what I had achieved. I began to notice that these subtle changes in me were also causing changes in the people around me. The more I grew, the more the people around me grew also.

The ripples spread far and wide and soon I was leading others down the path to this new and more productive mind set.

My blinkers had been taken off and suddenly I could see a whole new world surrounding me – one that I had not seen for a very long time. A world I had known as a little girl, full of promise, surprise and magic. The horizon stretched far and wide before me and I could see more clearly. The heavy fog of life's knocks and pessimism suddenly lifted.

My journey had taken me so far up to that point. I had experienced the highs and the lows with many obstacles, adventures and many successes. Gaining my Black Belt had been one of them, but as I sat there on that sunny afternoon I realised that achieving any level of success is simply a bench mark.

We should never stop growing or wanting to push ourselves to further limits, for it is only when we do - that we receive life's truest gifts - knowledge, enlightenment, vision and ultimately happiness.

This challenge proved to be my biggest gift from life so far. I knew that my journey was simply restarting in a whole new Technicolor - after all …..

*...a **Black Belt** is simply a white belt
who never gave up...*

Introducing you to the M.A.S.T.E.R™ System...

'Can you imagine what I would do if I could do all I can?'
Sun Tzu, The Art of War

Have you ever felt that life is getting the better of you and maybe.... you're finding it tough to fight back? Do you find yourself at times feeling despondent, depressed or lacking in self-motivation? Do you possibly feel overwhelmed, at a cross road, not knowing how to cope or what to do next?

If you have answered yes to any or all of these questions then this book will help you and I am guessing this is why you are already here, reading this right now. Well, first of all, let me tell you this. You are not alone. Many of us have been here, where you are right now; many are going through this with you, as you read these words. I also, have been here many times and this is why I am writing this book. To show you a way forward, to show you that it is possible to get back up, even when you are one hundred and ten percent sure that you can't. Even when you feel that you are not worthy, not good enough, not strong enough, not smart enough.

Whatever excuses you are making right now, I have said them also. I swear to you. You are just like me and I know all the excuses.

So this is what I will promise you right now. I promise to give you all I have got, but - you have to promise something also. You have to promise to do the same.

Now I know what you are saying. I hear you! I also had that niggling internal voice, but for now I just ask that you give yourself a break. Can you do that? Just tell that annoying voice to shut up and just keep reading, that's all I ask for now. The rest will follow.

I want you to hear my message first and foremost. I want you to hear it loud and extremely clear.

Imagine I am your mind coach, the sensei of your mind and I live in your head. Hear my voice screaming at you in your ear. Get up, fight back, and never give up!' Because that is what saved me and that is my message. And very soon that will be your message also, and it will resonate so loudly in you that the ripples will affect all that come into close contact with you.

This is the main message of this book –

To **never** give up.

Now I can hear you already. 'Yea, yea, that's all well and good BUT how do I do that?' If it was that easy then I wouldn't need to read this... right? - Right. Actually it's not so easy. Well it is and it isn't. It's always easy when we know how, right? - When we learn something - when we grow.

So that's what we will do here then. You will learn HOW. The principles are easy, the exercises are somewhat challenging at times, but I promise it will be a fun, exciting and enlightening journey for you.

What is sometimes hard is the time it takes us to become aware of how easy it is to be in control of our minds and our destiny. I plan to help you get to this awareness in a very short period of time, with the help of this book.

The following pages will recount the various obstacles and hurdles I myself, as well as others encountered throughout our lives and how we overcame them. The content you will read on these pages is the result of years of research, study and experience accumulated for the sole purpose of helping you to figure out your own mind and how to get a winner's mind-set.

If you are not getting all of the happiness or success you want in life. If your life is at a standstill or a cross roads, it is most likely because you are still doing the same thing, over and over, for a long, long time - what is comfortable, what is familiar, what you know and are used to - what you have learnt so far, up to this point. All your beliefs, responses and actions are due to past programming. Our brains simply 'automate' behaviour, unfortunately not always the right or most useful behaviour. But, obviously you can only work with what you have so far, what's in your box.

So what is in our box?
The sum of everything we know… so far.

Therefore it is hard to think outside of it, unless you either learn more or get out of your box. So what if you stepped outside? Then what? What if you pushed out of your comfort zone? If you keep doing the same, you will just get more of the same, right? … So what if you **'did'** differently?

The BlackBelt MasterMind is packed full of the most relevant cutting edge NLP, hypnosis and mind techniques (which I will explain more in depth in further chapters) and lots of exercises and fun tasks for you to undertake so as you learn all the facts about your brain and how it works.

The knowledge and experience I have accumulated from an NLP, Hypnosis, Business, Life and Martial Arts background has resulted in the creation of the M.A.S.T.E.R System, which is your ultimate step by step guide to becoming the Black Belt of your mind.

This book addresses the issues and pressures we all have today in modern society and explains how we have somehow forgotten that we are in control of our minds and not the other way around. We have allowed our minds to take over and hijack the controls of our ship. Here and now, you will learn how to take back that control and steer yourself in a new direction.

My aim is to get you to make the most of that wonderful computer that you have been given, so that you can go out and get all the success that you deserve.

You see, even though we may not always be fully in control of one of our worlds (*the external*), in the other world (*the internal one*), we are.

We have full autonomy and can choose our responses and in this book I will show you how to do just that.

Imagine your mind is like an iceberg. Let's say that seven per cent is above the water, on show. This is the part we see, the part we are more aware of, more familiar with – this represents our conscious mind. The other ninety three per cent is hidden below the surface. Undiscovered and unexplored, but still a very big and important part of the iceberg. In fact this section is holding the iceberg afloat and giving it support. This huge section represents the unconscious mind. This hidden and unseen area is the part we will be learning much more about as it dictates our everyday actions, moods and thoughts.

In 'consciousness', we are in a state of being aware and responsive to our surroundings. In fact we are always in a state of some sort. A state of calm, a state of anger or a deep relaxed trance-like state. Basically we traverse from one state to another. Our conscious or critical mind acts like a filter, limiting the information we have perceived to have taken in so that we don't get information overload.

But our unconscious in fact, has taken everything in, storing it for the future and those so called 'unusual' moments when you react a certain way, when you react out of certain old hardwired patterns.

In these chapters you will learn how you can change those patterns, habits and fears by rewiring your brain in a new way because luckily for us we possess the most incredible brain – a brain that is constantly evolving and ever changing. Yes changing!

Every time we learn something new, we create a new neural pathway, like a 'highway'. It's called Neuroplasticity and it means our brains are capable of growth and also of change. We can change the highways in our brain if we so want to. There is a way. We learn by repetition, over and over, until it forms its own pathway. The more this action, or thought, or habit is triggered, the bigger and more worn the street gets. But... what if we took a detour? What if we closed it off, made it a dead-end, causing us to double back down a different road, what then? Could we change patterns of a life time? Can change happen fast?

Let me ask you this instead. Have you ever picked up a habit, opinion or fear, in a matter of seconds? Think about it. Most of us have. The toddler fascinated by the fire, burns his little chubby hand on a piece of coal - previously curious, fearless and excited, now instead - cautious and a little wiser. Did he not change his opinion on that piece of coal fast? The young girl, who is constantly scorned by the good looking biker dude, runs out of the classroom to cry over her inability to be found attractive, only to overhear him talking to a friend about how much he likes her, but is too shy. Doesn't her perspective of the situation change, very rapidly?

We both know there are myriad examples that we could analyse, isn't there? Think about what you have learnt and changed in an instant. So then, if you can 'learn' a habit this quickly then what's stopping you from unlearning it just as fast? Aha, you see now your thinking - and that's the difference!

I have had the privilege of working with and learning from some of the greatest experts and geniuses of our time and I have since witnessed and partaken in many a transformation. My clients' testimonies are all the proof and inspiration I need to continue with my message that I am now sharing it with you.

Dr.Richard Bandler, the co-creator of NLP says, '*You can either react or think and plan..*' The choice is yours. You can either try and cope with the thoughts and feelings that are overwhelming you or you can plan and take action to move in the direction you want to go. The first process is called reacting and the second is called thinking.

In the martial arts world, this stage of simply 'reacting' is sometimes called the Tiger stage. The more enlightened, aware and knowledgeable we become the nearer we get to reaching the Dragon stage and ultimately our BlackBelt. How has the Tiger stage been working for you so far? We know deep down that our journey is only starting, at any given moment. We know that at this moment we have the power with our choices to change our circumstances. We know that it all lies in our decisions.

You decided to read this book and for that I want to thank and congratulate you. Thank you for giving me the opportunity to get to know you and to share with you what I have learnt. I would be humbled and very delighted to hear about your journey and transformation.

As a special thank you for being here, I want to offer you a special bonus.

Go to www.theblackbeltmastermind.com/bonuses to claim your well-deserved surprise gift. Your secret password is MASTER (In caps). You see you deserve it, because you are here, and that is why I would like to now say, congratulations to you!

Congratulations for taking this first step to be here. It shows you are aware. Aware that you want change and possibly need some guidance to get there. Not everyone realises this. Some keep trying to go it alone, but that path is much, much harder. The smarter minority realise that change will happen faster when you utilise as many resources as possible that are available to you.

Now in today's modern world those resources are abundantly available for you at the touch of a button. Information, courses, Skype calls, etcetera. Everything is there for you when you need it and you can see this where some others still don't. So congratulate yourself in taking this first step, even if you don't know what the next one is- yet.

It will become clearer as you read on, for we don't have to necessarily see the whole staircase, just each step as we take it.

Read this book how you will, fast or slow. I recommend doing both in that order actually, and then referring to this book any time you need to after that.

Most importantly, do the exercises with gusto, with soul. What I mean is, **feel the emotions as you do the tasks**. I cannot stress this point enough. This will help the process tremendously. When your mind recognises the emotion, it will store it as an eventful occurrence and file it away as more 'important', therefore keeping it in the more 'accessible' file drawer for you in the future.

Enjoy the feelings that come up and start experiencing the excitement that's yet to come. I know change is sometimes a little scary but the rewards, I promise you are truly worth it.

I am not here to pull you back from the edge. In fact, I am going to drive you over the edge, because that is the only way you are going to learn how to fly!

So…I dare you, to take action, right now, and let's get started on the rest of your life.

CHAPTER ONE

Beginning with the White Belt,
a blank canvas and how best to fill it...

'What we call the beginning is often the end
and to make an end is to make a beginning.
The end is where we start from.'
T.S. Elliot

From this moment on I will hold you as powerful, as special, as incredible, no matter what - even when you won't - because that is what I choose. I choose to be there by your side all the way until you reach the point where you don't need me anymore. I choose to be in your corner and to watch your back. I choose to cheer for you because I can see the greatness in you. And you can choose to see it too.

You see we always have choice and that means we can choose to do things we enjoy, spend time with loved ones, follow our passions or we can sit around and complain and blame others, the economy, our parents or the weather for our lives. You may not be able to just be happy but you can do things happily. That's your choice. 'Happy' is an adjective not a verb. We always have choices and those choices mean that you are capable of feeling more than one thing.

This means you have a choice on how often you want to do things happily.

Now I know you are still doubting me a little bit, fighting me with those negative, unproductive beliefs that are whispering in your ear saying things such as, 'yea but she doesn't know how hard it is for me. For me it's different because…bla di bla bla…'

I am not ridiculing these thoughts of yours; believe me, because they were mine also, once. I am simply saying I know that this is not true, I know this from knowledge and experience, that it is no different for you, and I will prove it to you with this book.

Once we take responsibility our lives begin to change but for now I will take the heat off you and start with how it all changed for me.

That summer's day, five years ago, when I sat on the floor and cried in front of all my staff, it was a turning point. I was lost, confused, and felt just like a deer caught in the headlights. I was shocked. How could this happen? I had been in business for over 16 years. I had run three successful restaurants and employed a small village of staff over this time. Of course looking back I can see all the signs, the ones I should have heeded (but that's for another book) and then there were the signs hardly anyone could foresee, the crash in the economy and the death of the Celtic Tiger and ultimately the death of my business and my life, as I knew it.

I told the staff to take what they wanted in lieu of their last week's wages, closed the doors on my third and last restaurant and went home, where I hid away from the world for the next few weeks. Burrowed under my duvet I didn't have to face the local gossip, the angry letters streaming through my letterbox or even my sorry reflection in the mirror. I felt a total failure and I did not have a clue what to do next.

Of course I had experienced adversity before in different ways and overcome it. My Italian father and my Irish mother had a turbulent relationship and my sister and I experienced many sudden nights of unexpected pyjama flights.

Finally, when I was nine, we took our last trip back from Rome and we moved into my Irish grandparents' home. They were different to my Italian relations. The culture was different. It was a little more restrained with emotions - quieter. I remember thinking everything was grey, most of all the weather! It took some getting used to but I did.

After some predictable banter over my funny Italian accent I finally started to make friends, but I never really felt like I quite fitted in. I always felt different as though I didn't belong.

Anyway, life went on. A further nine years later, when I was eighteen, I went over to see my papa again for the first time as a woman.

Soon after that I went to art college, but somehow in the midst of Gouache paint and Life Drawing classes, I ended up opening a restaurant with my now ex-husband.

Over the next fifteen years, I got married then divorced, experienced three automobile accidents, moved house a number of times, opened three businesses, earned my Black Belt and my European medals, fell in love, lost my two Newfoundland dogs, closed my businesses, struggled financially with overwhelming debt and was bullied and threatened by notorious gangsters..

To some this may seem like very little compared to what they have gone through, to others they instead ask me daily 'how do I do it?', 'How do I keep smiling?' I believe it is impossible to quantify the emotions we go through or to categorise them. I have learnt that it is always subjective.

I highlight my life story not for sympathy, nor to impress, but to simply impress upon you that we have all had good and bad experiences throughout our lives and I am no different. But, if it is all we have known and have experienced then it is what we feel and we can know nothing else. We are in our box and that is all we can deal with, of course.

So for me, when I closed my business I was lost. I felt alone, unsupported and sorry for myself and so I did just that. I wallowed in self-pity for a short while but the bills kept piling up and I knew, somewhere in the back of my fuzzy brain that I had to do something.

I knew if I stayed like this too long it would only get harder.

I would go down to my local village store to pick up some groceries and be met by curious stares and questions such as, 'Oh so you are still living in the town?' It seemed like such a weird question. Should I be ashamed? Should I scurry off with my tail between my legs? Had I really failed? Was 'I' a failure??

Something started niggling at me and I started to think.

I felt I had made a positive contribution to my local community. So why should I feel a failure? I read stories in the paper and on the news of how the economy was driving many to despair. Was I going to be a victim of this also?

Would I let my life be labelled by this? Was 'I' really just my business? Was I simply my job title or could what I 'did' be something more? Could it be what the results actually showed? What I contributed? I thought of what I had contributed so far and how much more I could actually do.

I heard the words screaming at me in my head. Get back up! Fight back! You have more in you to give! I realised what all those quotes and sayings actually meant and I finally understood them. If we keep on going, if we never quit, if we keep getting back up, then we cannot fail.

Success is defined in the dictionary as 'the accomplishment of an aim or purpose'. Failure is defined as 'lack of success'. What do these words mean to you? I define success as getting up one more time. That is my aim, to utilise what I have been given to its full capacity - to not waste my gifts. To follow my purpose in giving back all that I can in this world.

That is what winning means to me. Truly doing my best and never quitting. Have you done your very best yet? While we are on this earth we are still capable of giving back and letting our light shine. I decided to get back up and most of all to allow my light to shine.

Now, I know to some of you this might seem a little sentimental, corny even - but is that really what you think or is that just your social conditioning?

Is that what you are accustomed to hearing every day from the people you surround yourself with?

For if it isn't, then you better get used to it because you are going to start hearing a lot more of it and it would be useful if you start telling your friends, peers and loved ones also that this is what you are about to do.

Have you heard it said that 'we are the sum of the five people we spend the most time with'? How does that resonate with you? Well we will be spending a lot of time together now, so think about that.

Take a moment now to reflect on this before we start to shake things up for the better...

Do you like what you see?

Do you like the person that you have become?

If not, then it is time we changed this, so let's start with this inspirational poem by a remarkable woman...

'Our Greatest Fear'
by Marianne Williamson

It is our light not our darkness that most frightens us
Our deepest fear is not that we are inadequate.
Our deepest fear is that we are powerful beyond measure.
It is our light not our darkness that most frightens us.

We ask ourselves,
who am I to be brilliant, gorgeous, talented and fabulous?
Actually, who are you not to be?

You are a child of God.
Your playing small does not serve the world.
There's nothing enlightened about shrinking so that other people won't
feel insecure around you.

We were born to make manifest the glory of God that is within us.
It's not just in some of us; it's in everyone.

And as we let our own light shine, we unconsciously give other people
permission to do the same.
As we are liberated from our own fear,
Our presence automatically liberates others.

I really love this poem, and I hope you do too. I am not always so sentimental, in fact I prefer to deal with the pragmatic and we will - very shortly. However, I believe we need to allow ourselves to fell passionate about ourselves, to truly, honestly start to love ourselves, for this to really work.

Experience and time has shown that we tend to prefer to act as a collective, as a group or a pack. We like to just blend in as one of the sheep, so that we don't get noticed, for fear of being spotted and the wolf getting us. We have all heard the childhood phrase, 'Sticks and stones may break my bones but words will never hurt me'. Then why do we still feel so afraid? Why is the number one fear in the world public speaking?

It all stems from a deep rooted engrained fear, bred into us after thousands of years and based on our evolvement and survival mechanism. Now in the 21st century, we don't have to worry anymore, about the dinosaur or the tiger getting us. **_Our instinct has become extinct!_** This fear is now redundant! There are no tigers (*at least for most of us*) about to get us!

So when I ask you a question I once heard –

'Why do you try so hard to fit in
when you are born to stand out?

There are no more excuses.

You and I are both safe to do this now. We will survive under the scrutiny and the scorn of the less evolved and succeed in following our dreams to their conclusion.

So then, let's get started.
What is the first step in doing this?

In Martial Arts we always start with the basics and the same approach is wise with life. Without the basics it is harder to learn anything. Think of how we learn to read and write.

We start with the basics, the direction from which to read from, then the alphabet- a, b, c, and then we proceed to cat, mat, sat. Eventually we start creating sentences, the cat sat on the mat.

When learning the piano, we learn how to place our hands, the notes, then the chords and finally whole lines of music.

The same goes with Martial Art, we learn the basics, our stance, the principles of motion, then certain movements and then whole techniques. In this chapter we have already started with the basics of Stance.

When we teach new students about their Stance, we are helping them become aware of how they can master their own mind and body; this in turn will lead them to master all the various aspects that they want to create change, in their life.

This is the basis of my M.A.S.T.E.R™ System and leads us into the next Chapter where we will learn how to hone this skill and gain Masterful awareness.

N.B: Have you availed of your **FREE** surprise Bonus gift I mentioned in the Introduction? If you haven't yet, go grab it now at www.theblackbeltmastermind.com/bonuses and use your password MASTER.

CHAPTER 2

Yellow
'Masterful' Awareness and accessing our super brain...
Inspiring thought and inquisitiveness.

'Life's battles don't always go to the strongest or fastest man.
Sooner or later the man who wins is the man who thinks he can.'
Vince Lombardi

'Great moments are born from great opportunities' and that's what you have right here. This is where you really begin learning about yourself. Now is when you can start living rather than simply existing. This is the time for your massive action and it all starts with mastering your awareness.

When a White belt starts he is not aware. He is not aware of his body, of how he uses it or most of what is going on around him. He simply exists and moves instinctively through learnt patterns of motions, behaviour and understanding.

When we ask him for the first time to take a 'stance' his movement is awkward, cumbersome, as though he has suddenly forgotten how to use his limbs. He is either unsure and doubtful of his ability or he is so blinded by his false beliefs that he cannot see his own clumsy movements. In both cases he is unaware.

The instructor attempts to show him this but he doesn't see it. His reality, his map of the world, tells him differently. He 'imagines' that his own moves are identical to those of the instructor. The reality is very different.
So how do we find awareness?

We do it first by realising just like you are doing right now, that to master a skill we must first acknowledge that we may not quite have it —not just yet. The next step is simply to practice. By repetition, over and over just like 'they' say.

Repetition is the mother of perfection.

We find awareness by continually analysing what we do and what we say to ourselves – both the good and the bad.

Self-awareness is a very good thing. Once we know what we are doing then we have taken back control so that we can change it. We are not to judge ourselves harshly, for it is very normal that we may have fallen into some bad habits. It is self-awareness not self-consciousness we are striving to achieve.

When you become aware of the patterns then your brain knows how to look for them again. You will see the signs everywhere just like after you buy a new car and you then suddenly notice lots of others also have the exact same model as you! Part of your brain, which is called the Reticular Activating System, RSA, tells your brain what to notice.

Just like a special antenna searching constantly for the specific requests you have given it. We will learn more about this in a moment, but for now it is good just to let this information settle in.

This is an good point for you to keep in mind, for this gives you power, control and huge responsibility. 'A good thing?' I hear you asking. Yes, *response – ability* is a great thing to have! Once you have it you have the *ability* to choose your *response*. For you know that between every thought and action there is now a choice. **YOU choose how to respond**. So embrace *response-ability* and you will see the changes happening very fast, just like the colours on your Mind-Belt changing!

The yellow belt symbolises the tiger stage. The darkening of the belts represents the tigers brown stripes. Why are tigers striped? It can be camouflage against danger and also so as to sneak up on their prey. It is also a clear warning to others not to mess with them! In further chapters I will discuss the metaphoric transition you are making from the tiger to the dragon stage, but for now let's talk about rooting.

Interestingly, if we spell it as 'Routing', it is described as the process of selecting the best paths in a network. That's funny, because that is exactly what we are aiming to do here now. Choose the best and easiest ways for our most productive thoughts, moods and states, to reach our brain (our network) and thus help us achieve our goals

In martial arts terms, to root oneself is to form a stable, solid and secure base and also to tap into the natural energy of the earth so as to be connected and therefore be powerful. If you can't stand you can't fight. Every ethnic group and race has a power stance

The native American Indian, the Maori of New Zealand, the Maasai tribe in Kenya, all have a power stance and all realize the importance of the connection to the earth. The wisdom of the ages and the ancient chronicles speak of how this power stance connects us to the abundant energy of mother earth. Various cultures refer to this in many ways. We know it as Chi, Qi, Ki, Prana among many others but it is universally understood as the way to access your energy and your power through discovering our most basic stance.

Why do you think martial artists spend so long perfecting this stance? There are many peripheral benefits but the main one is to develop their connection with their Omni-present life force. When in this stance correctly, you will access a section of your brain that is not often spoken about in many self-help guides.

This largely unknown section is called the Reptilian brain, you may have heard of it as the Medulla Oblongata.

It is your primal brain or more accordingly for us it is your **super brain**!

Your super brain contains all the knowledge of your ancestors and your instinctual survival mechanism. It is your greater guide to your success and abundance in your life but it is rarely tapped. The fact that you are reading this is testimony to the effectiveness of this part of the brain. You are the sum of your ancestors and you contain all of their wisdom. Our basic power stance is not only relevant to physical power but more importantly it allows us to access the hugely powerful primal super conscious mind.

Have you ever had a frightening experience - maybe an accident of some kind? Did time appear to slow down for you? It is repeatedly reported and noted that in times of such stress that time indeed seems to distort. My own automobile accidents bear testimony to that and I remember having what appeared to be a lot of time to assess things, when in fact it was only a fraction of a second.

My Reptilian brain was momentarily awakened and I was able to see time in a new way. Just like a snake that can move with lightning speed when stalking its prey. This is because the snake does not think consciously, it is constantly in survival mode and that is what I entered. I was able to see time in a new way.

Our perception of time is simply all we know, the way we perceive it. It is our map, but as discussed earlier it is not necessarily the territory. The hummingbird that beats its wings impossibly fast, for us and our perception of time is still simply an everyday unconscious mechanism for the hummingbird.

There are many examples of when time appears to have been perceived differently. Many sports personalities often claim that when they are in the 'zone' that time has slowed down for them.

In the infamous boxing match between Steve Collins and Chris Eubank it was reported that Steve Collins used hypnosis, to help him slow down time so as to see his opponents punches coming at him – and he won!

Imagine now, how accessing this state will help you. People do it when they practice Yoga or Tai Chi or meditate and practice mindfulness. You too can start to access this super brain right now, through this simple exercise!

Learning how to breathe.
What? You know how to breathe already?

Most of us think we do and most of us have been doing it wrong all of our lives! Just to make sure you do know the right way, here are the steps;

- Slowly inhale through your nose to the count of 4.
- As you inhale make sure the tip of your tongue touches the hard palate behind your front teeth. As if you were about to say the letter L.
- Most importantly make sure, your stomach inflates as you breathe in. If your shoulders and your chest rise, than you are most likely shallow breathing and breathing incorrectly.
- Breathe out easily, again to the count of 4, through your mouth, allowing at the same time your stomach to deflate and your tongue to fall onto the base of your mouth.
- Repeat

N.B: *A side effect of breathing correctly might be you notice yourself yawning or feeling a little light headed. If this happens great, this is a good thing, as it shows you are finally getting that much needed oxygen to your brain, at last!*

Okay great, now we all know how to breathe; we can do Qi Gong, an old Tai Chi exercise used to access our super brain. I said earlier that these exercises have other benefits also. Doing this just 5 minutes a day will help with many issues, from stress and anxiety, to circulation, to back problems.

When we are in Qi Gong correctly our vertebrae touch and everything is aligned correctly for our Chi, our energy, to flow perfectly. The Chinese originally discovered this energy – this Chi in their search, ironically, for the best spots to strike someone and cause the most damage. When they found spots that seemed to have more effect they began to stick pins in these points on the body and when they struck other spots on the body, these needles would vibrate, tell-telling blockage points in the body, where energy had accumulated.

This was eventually how they started to create Acupuncture and figure out how and when your Chi/energy flowed best. In this exercise, discovered many centuries ago, you are allowing your Chi to flow fully and completely around your body, resulting in huge physical and mental benefits. It goes as follows:

Qi Gong exercise

- Stand with feet hip width apart
- Face toes forward with your toes very slightly turned inwards
- Leave a slight bend on your knees, so they are not tense, as though sitting on a high stool
- Balance your weight on the middle of your foot, around the inside of your ankles, not on the ball or heel of foot
- Hold your back straight, with stomach pulled in, but ever so slightly arch your shoulders forward, so that your back is in a very subtle C shape
- Hold arms out parallel to just under your nose
- Open your arms in slight semi circles, as though you are holding a large bouncy ball
- Face palms upwards and slightly inwards so you can see them
- Splay fingers apart but do not hold tense
- Imagine an orange under each armpit, so your arms do not drop down and touch your body
- Hold position for ten correct breaths
- Elongate your time each week until you can hold for five minutes

Note: After this, repeat for half the breaths again, this time with your arms parallel to your navel.

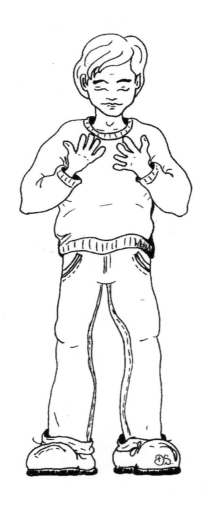

N.B: *As a special gift, so that you can learn this better, go to*
www.theblackbeltmastermind.com/bonuses/
to download your Bonus –
A very special video of me doing this Qi Gong stance just for you!
Remember your password ... MASTER (all caps)!

So now that you have started accessing your primal brain you might still be wondering how will that really help you? You see…everybody goes to the school of hard knocks once in a while but I am going to bring you now to the University of Abundance!

Firing your super brain through accessing your primal brain will result in many things; amongst others it fires your **Antenna of Abundance**. In this state you can access your Eagle vision, in other words seeing peripherally.

Let me give you an example….

At any point we have limited vision, right?

Lift your hand up and out to your side, on the same line with your ear, while looking straight ahead focusing on a spot in front. Now, you can't see your hand but you know it is there, right? How do you know? Because you have learned this and therefore you accept it. We have been blinkered and our vision is tunnelled simply because we are conditioned and told to look at things in a certain way.

If I now ask you to un-focus your gaze and don't stare at anything in particular, see if you can see your hand. You did, right?! This is simply because you allowed yourself to take in more information in a new way.

You see there is no real fact, only our interpretation of it depending on our focus.

Psychologists call this 'Inatentional Blindness'. There are many recorded and documented examples of very unbelievable cases where people passed by, focused on something else, and completely missed something very unusual occurring right before them. We don't notice what is happening under our very nose because we are focused on something else!

We can use to our advantage another scientifically recognised pattern that we tend to use very frequently. This is called our Confirmation Bias and we all use it a LOT.

I touched on it slightly in a previous chapter when I mentioned our Reticular Activating System and this is similarly related. Once we believe something our brain starts to search for this information elsewhere, so as to confirm what we already believe.

This is good for us to know as it means that what we 'believe' will become 'reality'. Our brain will do all that is possible to search, find and confirm. So then, doesn't it make sense to 'believe' in the good stuff?

Take off the blinkers, pull back the light and unfold the canopy behind so that the light shines all around. Start looking 360 degrees and know that there is opportunity everywhere.

To show you another example, follow this…

Look around right now for 5 seconds and notice everything that is red. Next, close your eyes. Now.....say out loud 10 things that are blue around you. Chances are you didn't do too well! Why??

Because we get more of what we focus on, right?!

So what is it YOU focus on? In fact, before we even start looking and examining what you see, I want you to concentrate on what you hear.

What is it that controls your thoughts, or who is it?

Who is that voice inside your head?

To gain **Masterful** awareness we need to start notice what it is we focus on and then change it so that we focus on that which we want to get. Makes sense, right? Right! So let's do it now...

Make a mental note to yourself to start right now to listen to your negative internal voice and what it is saying. NEVER judge it or of course then you are scolding yourself twice!

Just hear it. Listen to the tone, the pitch, the volume. Notice is it someone familiar, made up or even another you!

Now once you have discovered that you have this 'other' voice in your head do this exercise…

Exercise - 7 Days without negative thoughts! *[1]

Any time you hear your negative voice…simply;
Note it and say Stop or Shut up
(or anything else you deem more suitable!)
Repeat every time without judging

Over the next few days you will notice your negative voice silencing. You will notice yourself becoming more observant, beginning to access another state of awareness. In this state you are not only aware of the thought but also of yourself witnessing this thought. This brings you to a whole new level of consciousness and also helps you detach, disassociate from the thought, as you feel more removed, more like an observer rather than overwhelmed and drowning in it.

You are simply rewiring your brain and changing direction off well-used neural pathways. You are taking back control and teaching your brain that IT works for you and not the other way around. Otherwise our brains (*if allowed*) are automatically undisciplined, just like a badly tended garden with wildly growing weeds.

---

[1] * Based on the work of Dr.Richard Bandler

First we pull out the weeds (*our negative, critical voice*) and then we plant some new seeds to grow into flowers…

This leads us to the next chapter where we will learn how to fill our mind instead with sweet smelling bouquets of more productive thoughts.

N.B: Tip! Any time you feel down or absorbed in negative thought, keep your head pointing straight forward but look upwards towards the ceiling with your eyes. Keep your eyes looking up.

Harder to feel down? Yes, right! That's because you have detached/disassociated yourself from your feelings. You have removed yourself and taken yourself out of the overwhelming sensation.

Now.... you can start to think more logically!

CHAPTER 3

Orange
How to plant the seeds for the right Attitude

'Attitude is a little thing that makes a big difference'
Winston Churchill

It's not your aptitude
but your attitude
that determines your altitude!

An attitude problem always starts with a behaviour problem. Does that sound unusual? You see…we can't always see the attitude but we can see the behaviour. We develop attitude so as to explain the behaviour and this results in us always acting as if it is already true.

Primarily, it is a good idea to have started with discovering if we have an attitude or more specifically a negative or non- beneficial attitude. I am sure you are happy to keep any positive attitude you have! I am going to presume that you have taken heed of the last chapters and are by now becoming aware of any self-sabotaging ways you may have grown accustomed to and that negative voice that should by now, be hugely silenced.

So next, how do we cultivate the right attitude?

We start with what I promised you and an easy exercise to change our voice to a more pleasant one.

I call this…. **The Laurel and Hardy Exercise.**

The purpose of this exercise is to change the negative voice (*any time it tries to sneak inside your head*) to a voice that you cannot take too seriously, no matter how hard you try.

You see, when I grew up in Italy, Laurel and Hardy was dubbed of course, and they taped over the original actors voices with a stereotyped, very funny interpretation of what Italians believed an English accent sounded like. For me this was the funniest thing ever.

The Laurel & Hardy Exercise; *[2]

- Think of something that you keep feeling bad about and you are aware you are still talking negatively about.
  Rate how bad this voice causes you to feel, on a scale of 1 – 10. (10 = feeling really bad)
- Notice where the voice is coming from
- Notice who it is, the pitch, volume, speed, tone.
- Notice, if you see a person, what they look like.
- Now, change it completely.

---

[2] * Based on the work of Dr.Richard Bandler

- Imagine, that suddenly you could turn down the volume and simply white out that noise.
- In turn, turn up the volume on a funny voice that makes you laugh. This can be a person you know, a film star, a cartoon character, or even the imaginary voice of your favourite pet. It's your imagination, so use it. The sillier the voice and associated connection, the better it is for this exercise.
- Superimpose that funny voice on top of whoever it is speaking.
- Give them some funny ears, a red clown's nose and listen to that ridiculous voice now.
- Now, rate how bad you feel listening to this new voice, on a scale from 1 – 10. Better yes? YES!
- Repeat any time IF still necessary.

Okay, now that we have started changing our internal voice for a more productive one, how are we going to use it? How about we start to ask ourselves good questions? What do I mean by this?

Remember I said that we get more of what we focus on? Great! I am glad you were paying attention. So now think about this.

Do you have still have some negative thoughts, blocks, beliefs, bad thinking habits that are keeping you focused on the wrong thing? If you do, you need to look in the right direction. How do we do this? By asking the right questions – but first let's start with what's a really bad question to ask…. WHY?

Think of a young child wanting to get his way. He asks 'but why??' and gets a reply, only to ask 'but why?' to the new answer…and it goes on and on for eternity! So WHY do this to yourself?

Start noticing now, what type of questions you ask yourself and notice where the WHY question takes you. In terms of our mind and our decisions and our actions, we tend to always make these choices based on whether we are moving away from pain or towards pleasure. The WHY question will generally always bring you back towards pain, so WHY go there? Do you really honestly believe that knowing why will help you change something?

I believe in most cases that dwelling on the WHY only causes more suffering as it brings you straight back to the suffering. Once you start thinking or discussing WHY in most cases all you will do is re affirm and strengthen those well carved out neural pathways you have made. Have you not suffered enough? Do you really want to keep reliving it or bringing your mind back down to that negative state?

Start thinking rather than reacting out of habit.

You see our unconscious mind does not know the difference between what is real and what is imagined, if it did, then why do we often wake up from a dream, distressed, upset or feeling happy? Our unconscious mind did not know it was only a dream, it took it as a real event resulting in us feeling emotions.

So if we spend hours repeating past events, recalling upsetting circumstances or even imagining future bad scenarios our unconscious will believe we have done this, and give us the according emotion.

Make the decision today not to dwell on the WHY anymore as it points you the wrong way, towards pain and more of the same and not towards a solution. Decide today to note your verbal complaints and to start training your mind to think more productively.

Think about the last time you had a bad dream and woke up in a cold sweat or feeling emotional. How come you felt emotional if it was solely a dream?

55

Because as I said, your unconscious did not know the difference between what was real or imagined. So if you are going to imagine, than make it good, make it awesome and make it beneficial, because your unconscious is taking it all in!

Which leads me to this question. **What comes first?**

The Motivation = **ATTITUDE** or the Action? Generally we think motivation comes before actually doing, but is that entirely true? Think about something that you did well in, something you achieved, that made you feel great. Does that make you feel motivated to do it again? Of course! So, hence, the best process goes as follows....

Visualise = Achieving in your mind = Attitude/Motivation

N.B: Do this!

Try **not** to think about a pink elephant.

Did you think about a pink elephant?

I am going to presume you did, because the mind cannot process a negative. In other words for you to not think about a pink elephant your mind had to first think of it, in order to decipher what it's not supposed to think about!

What does this show you?

The more you say *don't think about something*, the more you will, because your unconscious will be constantly searching for it, so as to notice it and to alert you not to think about it! What a mess ay?? Therefore it is best to just allow the thought and acknowledge it, don't you think? ☺

When we visualise with real intent, with full emotion (*as I keep stressing*), then your unconscious believes you have done whatever you imagined already and hence you feel more motivated. Once again, makes sense, right!

If you are still stuck in the WHY and want to analyse it further, write down your answers to the following questions:

1) How much time everyday do you dwell on your problems? Write down an actual approximate total amount of time.
   Example; 2 hours a day._____

2) In what more productive ways could you use this time?

   _____

   _____

   _____

   _____

3) Concentrate on the WHY and Rate how you feel from 1 – 10 (10 feeling really bad)

_____

4) Rate how empowered you feel (1-10)

_____

5) Rate how strong you feel (1 -10)

_____

6) Rate how in control you feel (1 -10)

_____

I hope you are starting to get the idea....

Now... there is some benefit though in looking at the past, **albeit briefly and for a purpose.**

Sometimes we have to go on a round-a-bout journey to get to our final destination. Sometimes we have to go right back to the beginning for a brief moment and learn from our seemingly unusual path. Sometimes to find our spirit and our fire and our inner fighter we have to take a look at all the steps we took. I am reminded of the words of Morgan Freeman playing the part of a boxing coach in the film 'Million Dollar Baby'.

'Boxing is an unnatural act, everything in it is backwards.
You wanna move to the left, you don't step left, you push on the right
toe. To move right, you use your left toe. Instead of running from the
pain like a sane person would do, you step into it.
Everything in boxing is backward.
To make a fighter you gotta strip them down to the bare wood.'

Sometimes, we have to step into the pain to come out the other side so as to be able to see clearly what we have gained from the experience.

The following is a useful exercise, (*inspired by the wonderful Anthony Robbins*). This will help you gain insight into your strengths and thus improving your 'attitude' towards past unpleasant experiences. If you find that you are constantly saying that your past and your circumstances were shaped by outside sources and that someone else is to blame for how you are now, then this is for you.

I call it The Cause & Effect Game and it goes like this...

Cause & Effect Game

- Write down on a blank sheet of paper all the effects of whatever or whoever you blame, for your present circumstances.
- Keep writing until there is nothing else.

Example:
The economy closed down my business
The customers did not value my services
My parents did not show me enough love

- Once you have done that and felt all the emotion that went with it say goodbye and rip this up or even better burn it!

Now do this..

- Write down all the positive effects of these things that happened or that you believe

Examples;
My business closing proved to be the catalyst for my new found positive development
I learned valuable lessons about perception and perceived value that I have carried into my next business
I learned how strong I was and how much empathy I could now have for others

Now notice the difference in how you feel. Notice your new perspective – your knew attitude now that you can see all the positive effects that you gained from these experiences.

So now, getting back to **good questions**

The first stage to gaining a better and more productive attitude is by challenging your limiting beliefs. You do this by breaking down unhelpful thinking and asking better stuff so as to point you in the right direction. You see, believe it or not this book is not about simply 'positive thinking'. That's a cop out and something that anyone that has ever been feeling down can find extremely frustrating. There is nothing more patronizing or upsetting than a well-meaning person telling you to 'snap out of it' or 'think positively'.

The truth is this book as I said, is not simply about that, we know it does not work that way. The way it will work however is if you think more intelligently, constructively and artfully.

You are already starting to get the gist of this concept with what you have done so far here, now let's take it to the next level.

Once again, pick a negative belief that has been bothering you. One you find yourself stuck in and repeating the same mantra. Example; I am not good enough, pretty, clever enough, etcetera.

Your belief will determine your action and your action your results, therefore it makes sense to change our unproductive beliefs, right?....

So.. *What is stopping you?*

Give yourself a space and time to relax and write down your honest answers to these questions.

Artful questions for negative beliefs –

1) How do I know, for certain that I have this issue?

_____

2) Am I confusing a thought with a fact?

_____

3) Am I jumping to conclusions?

---

4) Am I overestimating the chances of disaster?

---

5) Am I thinking in an all or nothing way?

---

6) Am I using generalisation words such as always, everybody, and can I be sure of these words?

---

7) Am I concentrating and focusing more on the negatives rather than the positives?

---

8) Am I concentrating on my weakness rather than my strengths?

---

9) How did I cope with things in the past?

---

10) Am I assuming that this way of thinking is the only possible one?

---

11) How might someone else look at this?

---

12) What are the advantages and disadvantages of thinking this way?

---

13) How has this way of thinking served me so far?

---

14) Am I asking myself the best type of questions and if not what would be more useful? Am I asking WHY or am I asking WHAT can I do? Which is better for me?

---

15) What is stopping me right now from changing this belief?

---

16) What would I have to let go of, so as to also let go of this belief?

---

17) What pay-off would I have to give up?

---

18) What step can I take right now to start letting go of this belief?

So you see, our experience of the world is created by us, from the inside - and will result in our experience on the outside. This is what we mean when we use the expression, **'the map is not the territory'**.

Often, we make spontaneous decisions based on what we think is logical, based on what we think is fact, on what we have historically known.

But often what we 'know' is simply our reality and not necessarily true fact. It is unbeknownst to us based on what is called the 'availability heuristic'. What this simply means is we often base our decisions on the ease of memory to search for stored information to give us a result.

So, for example; If I ask you to think of the letter K. Do you think it is more likely to appear as the first letter in a word or as the third letter?

Any scrabble player will tell you that it is much easier to come up with words beginning with the letter rather than to think of words with the letter K in the third position. So therefore, immediately more words starting with K spring to mind. It is the same with any letter of the alphabet. We all generally say the latter, in first position, as it is quicker for our mind to search for the result. Not always the correct one - a good point to keep in mind. Nobel Prize winner Daniel Kahneman discusses this in his fascinating bestseller book, 'Thinking, fast and slow.'

When we start to think productively and ask good questions we then start to get different answers! More useful answers and hence we can change our attitude and thus our results.

Many of our thoughts are like candyfloss, they evaporate once you bite into them.

If we fill our mind with thoughts of scarcity, lack, anger and jealousy, we will undoubtedly feel pretty miserable. If we choose instead to repetitively concentrate and focus our thoughts on abundance, creativity, courage and love we will automatically feel better! It makes sense.

What have you been filling your mind with?

I remember a time when a sad song would come on the radio and I would automatically turn it up and by the end of the song I would be wailing to it. Maybe you can relate to this. It was like a drug, I needed it so badly. I would, in fact, search for the saddest songs!

I also remember the day, when I was on my journey of self-discovery that I recognised this, just as my hand reached to turn up the soppy song on the radio. I stopped mid track (excuse the pun). I realised how difficult it was for me to stop myself and I also noticed what it was I wanted. I wanted the pain! It helped me feel alive.

Now that may sound weird and in fact even strangely annoying to some, you may even feel angry at me saying this. I was. When I was told that I enjoyed wallowing in self-pity I was defensive and very angry. *No, I wasn't doing this by choice!* I wailed. *Why on earth would I do that to myself?*

But as I reached for the volume dial I realised they were right. I stopped and thought about what I gained from it. What the pay-offs were. This was the crux of it. I was horrified!

I wanted to feel a victim because that meant I could continue the way I was without taking responsibility for it. Changing the channel to a happier song was excruciatingly difficult!

Over the years I have weaned myself off this and watched it carefully. Now I notice if I am going down that path and only listen to music that inspires and uplifts me. I also would recommend the same for any information that you take in, that is not beneficial, like any unhappy news or media - As they say... *'rubbish in, rubbish out'.*

So remember to fill your mind with productive, good thoughts, and remember that, **'The map is not the territory.'**

There are numerous examples I could give you but I will share with you the following, as I am a big animal lover.

When a baby elephant is first trained by a circus trainer, he is often tied to a small post so as to keep him from running away. The little baby elephant tries hard to free himself but he is too small and can't break the little post. He tries and tries and tries but eventually gives up, knowing there is no point. Time passes and the little elephant grows much larger, but – the post stays the same size.

Soon the little post is clearly as fragile as a twig against the giant strength of the huge elephant. The circus trainer knows this but isn't bothered, as he has seen this many times before and knows that little elephant is completely unaware.

The Elephant has made the Map his Territory.

This sad metaphor has many messages; I hope you can see some of them now.

To end this chapter on Attitude we will do a wonderful exercise, to get you in the right frame of mind, before we continue onto the chapter on Strength.

Think of someone, real or imagined that you admire and believe has a wonderful attitude to life that you aspire to. It can be a family relation, a film star, a famous person or a fictional character from a movie.

Read this through, so you know the steps and then close your eyes and do the exercise.

Exercise - Your new Attitude enhancer! * [3]

- Sitting in a quiet place, undisturbed, close your eyes.
- Imagine that person in front of you now.
- Watch them as if they are only a foot in front of you.
- See how they carry themselves, what they say, how they gesture and use their hands. Their facial expression and their body posture.
- Now, stand up and as you do so imagine you are stepping into them.
- Feel yourself absorb all the qualities that they have as you merge into one.
- Enjoy this as you start to learn what it is like to be them and to gain knowledge from this experience.
- Notice all the things that you can take from this, how you are now moving differently, carrying yourself and behaving. How your muscles in your jaw feel. How awake and alert you feel. Notice also what you are now saying to yourself being this new you. Notice what you think and how you speak, react and plan from this new perspective.
- Step out of them carrying with you all you have learned from this.
- Sit back down and reflect on what new knowledge and attitude you have brought with you and now carry.

---

[3] * Based on the work of Dr.Richard Bandler

N.B: *If you think you are struggling to visualise or that you cannot do it properly, do this. Close your eyes. Think of what colour your couch is. That was visualization. You had to see it to get the colour. If it's not exactly like real life, that's okay. It means you're not crazy!* ☺

71

CHAPTER 4

Inspiring higher ideals with Purple Strength

*"You have power over your mind - not outside events.
Realize this, and you will find strength."*
Marcus Aurelius

Strength is like a muscle. It gets stronger the more it is used. It also comes from adversity, big and small. Continually pushing your boundaries and facing your fears will build that strength muscle so that you can overcome anything.

In the last chapter we addressed how to build a more empowering and useful attitude and we looked at how to break down limiting negative beliefs. This firstly created doubt in your old ways, and then opened up a space for you to fill with a more useful attitude.

Now is when we will elaborate further on this so that you can gain massive strength and confidence from your new beliefs. Just like we exercise our physical body to build our strength, we must do the same with our mind.

Experience has shown that for us to be at our ultimate peak strength and performance we need first to be aware that we possess two sides to our minds and to unite the two.

In brain terms we can call this our logical and our creative brain, our left and our right, if we learn how to use both fairly equally or be able to tap into each when necessary this is very useful.

In martial arts terms we call this the Scholar and Warrior principle – Uniting the person. It is all that we possess inside. We possess both the scholar - our intellect and the sum of all we have learned. This is represented by our left open hand. Our warrior - holds our intuition, our instinct and our survival and fighting spirit in our right closed fist. You can only be at your most magnificent when your... *'Scholar and warrior go forth together, to battle back to back, to pull your life together'. ***

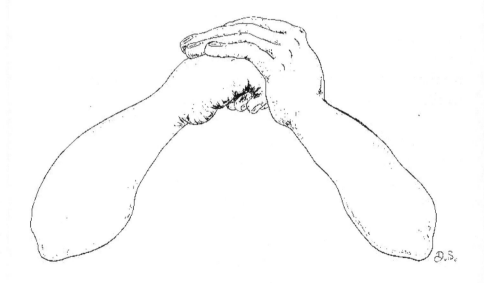

* Based on Ed Parker's Kenpo Salutation.

73

This is the basis of our martial art creed but also the basis of this chapter. To gain optimum strength you need to access and pull together all of your inner resources, your intuition, your instinct and all that you have learnt up to this point.

The following is an adaptation of a well-known NLP exercise called the Visual Squash *. I call it 'The Scholar & the Warrior' Exercise and it will help you tremendously to build strength and courage in your life.

As already stressed previously the more you can 'feel' in these exercises the better for you. When you really live these experiences using all your senses, so that your unconscious accepts it as an event, this is when real neurological shifts begin to happen.

This exercise will help you gain clarity and a positive intense state for any goal that you want to achieve and therefore the strength to pursue it. It will bring you from a state of uncertainty and weakness to a state of clarity, confidence and strength.

Exercise - The Scholar and the Warrior * [4]

1) Create an image of yourself now, as you are, in your present state, with all your current problems.

---

[4] * Based on the work of Dr.Richard Bandler

Imagine placing this image in your left open hand, your scholar, your past and the result of all you have learnt up to this point.

2) Now create another image, using all your senses. Imagine the new you of the near future. The strong, powerful you who has the courage and the strength to achieve any goal.

See all the details, how you are behaving, what you are saying, feeling, hearing. Make it as real as you can until your hair stands on end with excitement.

Imagine placing this image in your right hand and then wrap your hand into a fist as you hold all that power within it.

3) Holding your arms outstretched, look at the space between your two hands. This space represents the gap, the space in time unexplored, and holding the unspecified steps to help you reach your goals.

4) Begin to imagine the logical steps between the two states (your two hands). Create images or movies of the stages in this space to bring you from your current state to your desired state. Keep adjusting and working with each picture until you have formed a clear and progressive process for all the steps, to lead you from one hand to the other.

5) When you have all your stages, look at them and then slowly begin to bring your hands closer to one another, in so doing collapsing all the stages together, like a domino effect, into a single process.

6) Connect your hands by wrapping your left open hand (*your Scholar*) over your closed right fist (*your Warrior*), feeling as you do the power of that connection and all that you pulled in between.
7) Pull your clasped hands towards your body, feeling as they connect with you all this new empowerment and strength surging through you.
8) Allow this wonderful feeling to spread throughout your body so that all your muscles and fibres are now twitching with anticipation and excitement to take action and pursue this goal. As you allow these feelings to engulf you, look back on the steps you seen in the empty space between your hands and decide clearly what you have to do first.
9) See yourself now, standing up and taking the first step, then the second and so on, until you feel so compelled that you want to do it right now and go and take action!

Okay, now that we have improved our strength muscle, let's look at how we can use it and what is the one thing that generally stops us from moving forward. Do you know what it is?

A small four letter word that keeps us often paralysed. Once we understand it, we then have the power and the choice to deal with it. Let me spell this word out to you this way....

False Evidence Appearing Real

Now, this may be a bit of a generalisation, as of course sometimes our fear (I am presuming you figured the word out) is actually justified. If a tiger is chasing you or you are hiding from an intruder, your **fear** may indeed be considered natural. So let's take a quick look at these rational times first and examine how fear truly affects us.

Going back again to our pre historic times, fear was there to help us. Imagine you are in the jungle. Your brain processes a potential threat, let's use the tiger, and it alerts your brain of danger. Your brain in turn puts your body into an emergency state which then causes you to react in a certain way, starting with the Fight or Flight response.

Your body is at this point flooding with adrenalin and the blood is being pushed to your major muscle groups, your limbs or where your brain has decided you need it most. All other organs temporarily slow down, so that the maximum energy can be pushed to your limbs to either fight or flight. If you do not react, by either fighting or running away, you will then, very soon, be paralysed by the adrenalin that has now engulfed you and you will become a tasty meal for the tiger.

This reminds me of one of my favourite martial arts quotes... ☺

'He who hesitates, meditates in a horizontal position.'
Ed Parker Founder of American Kenpo

The same is true in life.

When faced with a decision and taking action, **inaction can be paralysing**. The more you practice NOT doing or moving forward the more you will stay in the same position.

Luckily for us, most of the time we are faced with a threat it is often not a serious danger, hence the phrase, False Evidence Appearing Real. Even still, doing something in these situations is generally better than doing nothing.

Once again, to reiterate, if we want to build our strength muscle we have to train it. We can start to do this immediately by taking action and making decisions every day. Research shows that people that make small decisions quickly and easily every day are able to take more important action quickly and easily when the time is needed.

Our brain appears to be aware that we are making all these small decisions and so has learnt to trust us; we in turn learn to trust ourselves also. When the time comes that we have to make serious decisions or take vital action, we have built up this strength and decision making muscle, and our brain knows it and obeys our command without questioning it.

N.B: Start to take notice of all the little generally unimportant decisions that you procrastinate and deliberate over.

Next time you are deciding what to eat at a restaurant, make the choice quickly, without regret. Most likely it won't be your last meal! Next time you have to choose a film to go and see, pick one with ease, you can always see the other one next week.

Don't sweat the small stuff
and the big stuff will be easier!

Fear, will never go away unless you face it. Pushing through it will leave you feeling empowered; doing nothing will leave you helpless.

We often prefer to stay paralysed in one place because of what is our biggest instinctual draw. This draw holds us prisoner and stops us moving forward. This draw is called the FAMILIAR. Sound familiar at all? ☺

Unfortunately, our urge to stay in the **familiar** also stems from pre-historic times. Our urge to huddle in our little well known cave is very enticing. We know all the nooks and crannies, all the grooves in the rocks and we love our prided pre historic rock art! The important point to remember, once again, is that, we have moved on and evolved from those times and we now no longer have the same threats and dangers that once lurked outside the safety of our cave.

We can now step outside our cave and face the unknown.

Our fear of the unknown is generally overrated and this is where we now need to pay special attention to our useful phrase- *False Evidence Appearing Real.*

Once again, stepping out and facing this unknown, every day in little ways will strengthen your muscle. Start to take little steps into the great unknown, every day. I am sure, from experience, you have many times in the past stepped outside the familiar, outside your comfort zone only to realise that it was never as bad as you thought it would be and often is in fact a bonus. The act of stepping outside your comfort zone will help you grow. Think of the Japanese Koi fish. When in his little tank he remains small, but once let out to swim free in the lake he suddenly grows. His growth is proportional to where he lives and while he lived in the bowl he never even knew the lake existed.

Go outside and find your lake!

Become aware of when you are generalising, when you are blowing things out of proportion. Use your artful questions to break down your limiting beliefs and evaluate if the evidence that appears real is in fact false.

Now before we go and do the next exercise, let's talk a little more about NLP. Aha, you have noticed! We haven't really discussed it at all, have we?

Actually, we have, but not in the way you may think we have - for I planned this book, this way!

If I had started with a longwinded explanation of what NLP was, it may have seemed daunting, overwhelming, or even simply boring – because, you're not here to learn about NLP, or are you? You are here because you want help and clarity to get your mind working more efficiently for you, right?!

Well, that is what we have been doing so far, and that is pretty much NLP. You see, NLP stands for Neuro-Linguistic Programming, in other words, the language that we use to programme ourselves and others. Yes, programme. Is that a good or a bad thing? Are we simply just like robots? Yes, kind of, BUT we are the only robot that can self-programme itself, how cool is that!

The term NLP was created by two men named Richard Bandler (whom I have had the honour of training with) and John Grinder. They spent many years studying and observing other experts in their field of psychology, psychiatry, and anything related to the mind.

They started to notice certain trends and patterns in what worked and how these experts were getting the best results with their clients. In fact these experts were just using instinctually and through experience the tools that worked best for them. The accumulation of this research was what became coined as NLP.

In fact we all use 'NLP' every day. Even before we had heard the term, even as little children, we used NLP.

Whatever terminology you want to give it, whatever name, it is all the same thing - useful thinking and useful communication; both with ourselves and with others.

Think of the last time that you made eye contact with someone, or smiled at them. Why did you do this? Whether you choose to admit it or not, this was a form of instinctual and learnt behaviour. We do this every day. We manipulate people every day for our benefit - sounds quite controversial but it is true.

Think about how you interact with others and when you behave in certain ways and be honest with yourself, as to why you do this. Generally it is for a gain of some sort. Maybe, it is to be liked, to fit in, to gain approval, recognition, validation, etcetera, but always it is for a gain.

NLP is simply a title for a way of life, a metaphoric tool that you can learn to hone and develop, so as to aid and steer you and also others in the path that you want to go.

So now that you understand this concept, in its simplest form, we can continue onto honing this skill and setting the path in the direction you so choose. We will do this first by learning how to rid ourselves of that horrible word FEAR so as to gain more STRENGHT, with one of my favourite technique

Think of something that has been holding you paralysed, static, stuck in a place of fear –

An event from the past, a phobia, or even an imaginary frightening scenario. Now get comfortable in a chair, with no distractions, for we are about to watch a spectacular movie and gain the wonderful benefit of ridding ourselves of this terrible fear.

I Like to call it..

Your Directors Cut * [5]

- Get comfortable, close your eyes and take a deep breath and relax.
- Imagine you are sitting in the middle of the front row of a beautiful movie theatre all by yourself.
- The plush red velvet curtains start to pull back as the music starts.
- On the crackling screen in front a Black and White Movie starts.
- The title of the film appears and it is your name followed with the words, 'Overcoming my old fear of...... (Fill in the blank)
- Watch the movie begin from your safe spot in your seat.
- See the YOU on the screen and watch that Black and White crackling movie of the event that happened that caused you such fear or the first time you remember being held by that fear.

---

[5] * Based on the work of Dr.Richard Bandler

- Watch the movie to its conclusion until the credits appear and the curtain is pulled, from your seat, observing how this other you looks and behaves from this detached, disassociated position.
- Notice if you feel any fear in your body from this safe place.
- If you do, imagine yourself now, floating out of your body and floating upwards and into a seat in a balcony above. Watch the YOU that is sitting watching the movie below and notice how much more relaxed you feel from here.
- Now, I want you to imagine some very funny music, something like Benny Hill or funny Circus music.
- The Movie starts again, but this time in reverse.
- The funny music is playing loudly and the film crackles into life, starting with the ending credits.
- Watch the movie running backwards, superfast, like a funny Charlie Chaplin movie in reverse.
- See yourself moving backwards and the event happening super-fast. From the moment you see yourself looking frightened to going back to the moment before the event happened and you are perfectly calm and happy.
- Stop it. Freeze frame it on the moment before the event and look at your happy, relaxed expression.
- Now repeat this exercise 5 times. Start at the end, at the credits and rewind back superfast, with the funny music all the way back to when you freeze frame on your happy expression.

- Now, I want you to float back down into your body sitting in the front row.
- Now imagine yourself standing up and walking and stepping up and into the screen, which is freeze framed on your happy expression.
- Step into the happy YOU on the screen and bring it suddenly to life. This time make it full techno-colour, bright and beautiful
- See yourself handling this event with a new-found strength and confidence. See the positive outcome and relish in how good you feel. Be in this new and much more productive state. Live the movie fully until the new and improved conclusion, enjoying immensely how you handled the experience this time.
- Step out of the movie and float back into the 'you' in the front row, carrying with you all the wonderful new feelings and insights out of this new found outcome.
- Feel how strong you feel as you open your eyes and bring yourself back into the room.
- Now, try and recall how bad you used to feel thinking about this experience, and notice how the fear has hugely diminished or gone completely!

The End...

To say another special thank you for being here and taking the steps to change your life, I want to offer you another Special Bonus.

Go to www.theblackbeltmastermind.com/bonuses to receive your FREE Gift – Password MASTER I know that sometimes at the start learning how to guide yourself through these processes can seem a little daunting, so I have a recorded a download for you, of me talking and guiding you through this exercise. Enjoy!

So, to end this chapter, and before we continue with 'Tenacity' ☺, I would love you to decide to follow through with the task below. I promise it will be fun and the rewards spectacular! Do it and watch your world change.

The FEAR Buster!

Task

Pick a comfort zone breaker

1 for every day of the next week
Write a list and do 1 a day!
Tick off as you do!

Step Outside of your comfort zone and become OUT-STANDING!

CHAPTER 5

Blue - Tenacity

'Tomorrow is often the busiest day of the week'

"That which does not kill us makes us stronger."
Friedrich Nietzsche

To think long about thinking
often becomes its undoing.

Stop thinking and start doing! You now know that if you don't take action you will freeze, but unfortunately sometimes this is not enough, as we still don't have that tiger salivating at our heals, to motivate us to take action! So how do we motivate ourselves to go after what we want? How do we develop that Tenacity??

We already know that Visualising helps this process immensely, because your unconscious does not know the difference between.....................................or
...................................?

I am presuming, you knew how to fill in the blanks above. Well done! So now, it is time that we start to fill in the blanks also for your unconscious. So as to help you gain the tenacity to reach your goals. Watch out, exciting times ahead!

If our brains are primarily run by our unconscious, and our conscious plays a much smaller role, then it is clear that many of or decisions and actions that we think happen 'spontaneously' are in fact affected and hugely influenced by other factors - previous experiences and events plus the accumulation of all that our unconscious has taken in. No wonder so, that we sometimes find ourselves acting or reacting strangely and what we think is out of context!

In fact, we make somewhere between 2,000 and 10, 000 decisions a day, most of them without even consciously being aware we are making choices. In scientific terms, these two Systems (our Conscious & Unconscious) are described as our Slow and Fast Systems. Our Slow System, is our Conscious – our Logical, deliberate part, the one you use when you hear that voice in your head. This part involves concentration and effort. In fact when you use this part (your conscious) your physiological state changes. For example, your heart rate speeds up and your pupils dilate.

If you want to see how this actually plays out, have a go at this ☺ Stand up and start to do jumping jacks. Now, count backwards, minus 7 numbers each time, from 10,000. Now stop jumping (*if you have not already*) and see if it is easier to do while still. Yes, right! That's because it requires conscious concentration.

Our other System is the fast one. It appears automatic and effortless. This is because it is our Unconscious and therefore holds our learnt responses.

It is wise for us to pay attention and note this information and to spot that many of our decisions are based on previously stored information. This means that our decision making process is not always logical.

This is called the Anchoring Effect. This is when you make decisions based on previous decisions – not always the wisest ones. Therefore, it is good for us to remember this at times when we need to make important decisions. Delay the impulse (our unconscious response) momentarily, and analyse logically, with our conscious mind.

This requires a certain amount of discipline, strength and tenacity and here and now is when we start to tap into this tenacity you have.

The first thing that you need, if you want tenacity, is to know what you want it for. Sounds obvious, but many clients say that they do not know what they actually want. Do you?

If you got into your car and started it right now and just started to drive, would you know where to go to? Do you know? You may not, right? Because, how can you know your destination if you have not planned it first?

So the first step, in deciding what it is that you want is to plan and we do that by….. yes, visualising once again!

But here is the catch.

If you simply start imagining solid, inanimate 'stuff', that serves no direct purpose, your unconscious won't be fooled that easily. Instead imagine what would you be doing if you felt happy, ecstatic, content, at peace, whatever emotion you prefer to use.

Now, what are you doing?

In other words, instead of imagining the end goal, let's take having lots of money as an example, and you visualise counting it. You could be working in a bank! Instead imagine the consequences and the effect of having this money.

In fact ironically, you ask the question;

What would I be doing right now if money was no object??

So....

What would you be doing now?
What does this mean for you?
What would that mean for your life?
What would that mean for the people you love?
What could you do if you had this?
What effect would it have on the people you love?

You see, this type of visualising and smart questions, will lead you to what is your real purpose. This is how you find it. Once you find your purpose you will automatically find your **Tenacity**.

Viktor Frankl speaks about this in his emotional but deeply inspirational book, 'Mans Search for Meaning'. Throughout the most harrowing, horrendous and unimaginable experience he went through as a Jewish prisoner in the Holocaust, he kept himself sane and alive by knowing his purpose. This kept him strong and gave him the tenacity to know that they would not break him and that he would overcome and be able to spread his message to others.

His book touched me greatly, and I feel humbled to be able to somewhat share his message here and now. Most of us have not gone through what this man has, but we still possess inside of us this huge untapped potential to make a difference every day, to your life and that of others. Every day you have this opportunity.

At any given moment,
you have the choice to stand up and
be **Masterful**,
change your **Attitude**,
find your **Strength**,
discover your purpose
and with all your **Tenacity**
go out and make a difference.!

So let's start this now with learning how we do make decisions and how we strategize.

We don't generally have the tiger at our heels, so what is it that pushes us forward or holds us back?

If it is not Fear that is stopping you, then what is?

It could very likely be what we call the....

Pleasure - Pain Principle.

We are always either moving towards pleasure or away from pain. Knowing what we are more enticed by, gives us more choices to use it to its full extent. Allow me to elaborate...

Everybody that says they can't be motivated goes out and does other stuff! - This means that they CAN be motivated.

It simply means they have associated and linked a pleasurable outcome to the things they are motivated to and an unpleasant outcome to the things they do not feel motivated to do.

Think about this now;

- Write down 3 things that you feel easily motivated to do.
- Now write down, what outcome you first think of.

Example; You feel easily motivated to eat chocolate.
Outcome =You immediately think of a pleasant sweet sensation and a deep sense of relaxation.

Now do the opposite –

- Write down 3 things you feel unmotivated to do, but would like to feel more Tenacity towards.
- Now write down what outcome do you associate with it.

Example; You would like to go jogging but feel unmotivated.
Outcome =You immediately think of sweat, pain and heavy limbs.

Mmmm, not that motivating, is it? Or that smart!

Unfortunately many of us do this all the time to ourselves and then wonder why we then can't motivate ourselves. We self-sabotage our goals. Richard Bandler says;

'Disappointment takes adequate planning',

And it seems we often appear to plan, very well, to fail.

If a tiger came running up to you now though, or if I pointed a gun at you and told you to run, I am pretty sure you would. This is because your Pleasure-Pain chart reached a tipping point. The act that you had been avoiding by associating pain to it, has suddenly now become more pleasurable than staying where you are!

This tipping point is what we need to reach when we want to motivate ourselves.

- Write down again the 3 things that you most want to achieve.
- Now write down a list of associated pleasures you can bring to doing this task.

  Example; I want to go for a 30 min run every morning.

  Pleasures: Rewarding myself with a healthy, tasty smoothie on my return. Taking an invigorating shower with my comforting shower gel. Showing off my new state of the art trainers.

- Imagine the benefits to your life in 1 years' time, if you do this now.

Keep looking for ways to associate pleasure to the task you want to do and eventually you will reach your tipping point, rolling you down the hill towards pleasure and taking action.

Your only limitation is your imagination and that is limitless.

Knowing what strategy we use and if we often run away from pain, is also useful. Think of something that you procrastinated about for a long time (*in other words, you associated a lot of pain to doing this*). Now, think about when you finally took action.

What changed? What made you finally get up and take action? …..You had reached your tipping point. The balance had changed to the other side. Now instead, staying in this place of doing nothing was proving more painful.

You had started to associate more pain to <u>not</u> doing!

How can you use this information?

- Think of something you would like to do, but have not done yet.
- Focus on the consequences and the pain of staying the same and not doing anything.
- Imagine your life in 1 years' time if you do nothing.

You see, to have Tenacity and to experience consistency, you need to be consistent! Fairly obvious….once we become aware of it. Which you are by now, I am assuming. You have noted previously in this book how much wasted time you spend on unproductive, detrimental thoughts. You know you can use that time much more wisely now. So what are you going to think of instead?

What would you like to achieve that you have not felt that motivated about doing? Let's do this exercise, one of my favourite.... I call this....

Exercise - 'The Elephant and the Mouse' * [6]

- Get comfortable and close your eyes.
- Think of something that you really want to change, an action you want to do, but have not had (up to now) the motivation and Tenacity to go after.
- Look at the image (your 1st image) that comes to mind, when you focus on this action.
- Notice all the details about it;
  How big the image is.
  Is it in colour, or black & white, or just grey.
  Does it have a border or a frame or is it endless.
  Is it close or far away?
  Is there any sound or smells associated with it.
  Are you 'in' the image or are you looking at it.
- Now, bring to mind something that you have achieved in the past, (2nd image). Something that you are proud of and made you feel good. Something you felt very determined to do and you did. It can be something very simple, as simple as deciding to cook a nice meal and going and doing it and achieving it. Of course, the more emotive and the higher the feel good factor the better.

---

[6] * Based on the work of Dr.Richard Bandler

- Once again, pay close attention to ALL the details.
- Now, imagine you are sitting at a desk with a computer screen in front of you. Place your hand on the 'mouse'. (Or the mouse pad on the keyboard)
- In a moment you will click the 'mouse' with your finger, and when you do, the 1st image will shrink down, just like when you reduce a computer screen.
- At the same moment a new big screen will open up, with **the action you want to do <u>BUT</u> it has all the details you noted from your 2nd image. (The one you felt good about).**
- Now repeat this exercise 5 times or until it is too difficult to find that original 1st image.
- Open your eyes, take a deep breath, think of the action you want to go do now, and notice how good you feel!

"You have brains in your head,
You have feet in your shoes,
You can steer yourself in any direction you choose.
You are on your own and you know what to do now,
You are the guy who'll decide where to go."

Dr.Seuss

Now, that you are feeling much more Tenacious, it is best to continue to use that focus wisely. You are going to plan out the next 30 Days on your Winners Path to Success!

Get a BLUE pen (*your brain recognises this colour as more important than black*) and start to fill out the below ☺

30 Day Winners Path to Success!

My Daily Affirmation....

I am.... _____

_____

_____

_____

(To be said EVERY morning
while looking in the mirror and SMILING)
N.B: *Even if you don't feel like it and feel pretty stupid, when you*
smile your brain will recognise that the muscles in your face have moved
into a smile position and will be fooled into thinking you feel happy,
kindly sending a gush of serotonin to your brain.
So keep doing it and you will feel better!

My 30 Day Goal
Now, write out in as much detail as you can
your ultimate goal of 30 days from now.

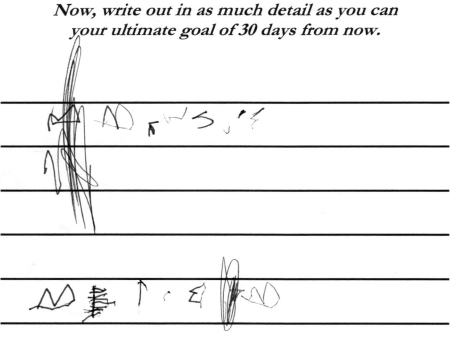

My Daily Gratitude list
Write out every night before bed, just before you sleep, 5 things for which you are grateful for.

_____

_____

_____

_____

_____

1 Thing that I will do today to improve my relationship with…..

_____

_____

_____

_____

1 Thing I will do today for my family or my friends…..

_____

_____

_____

_____

1 Thing I will do today for myself……..

_____

_____

_____

1 Thing I will do today for my growth and learning…..

_____

_____

_____

_____

1 Thing I will do today to contribute towards society...

_____

_____

_____

_____

1 Thing I will do today to get me closer my goal...

_____

_____

_____

_____

**Every day for the next 30 days,
do these exercises and pay close attention
to the changes that start to happen….. ☺**

For me…

*Manifesting your destiny is very much like painting a picture.
You begin with some inspiration,
add a splash of imagination,
which gives you the motivation to create your own masterpiece.
Then it all becomes reality by your own actions
and your choice of brushstroke.*

Pick a bright colour and bring your dream to life.

CHAPTER 6

Green for calm and wellbeing
Equilibrium EQUALS Balance

'A shadow cannot exist without light'

In the year 1557 a Welsh mathematician called Robert Recorde invented the 'equals' sign (=). He was inspired to use it as a means to a shortcut with his mathematical equations. He based it on the idea of the 'Genove' lines = the twin lines, stemming from the Latin word Gemellus.

The word equals comes from the word equality, meaning a person or a thing that is the same as another. It means the 'same as'. This, can have many meanings I believe. It comes from the Latin word 'Aequus', which translates as level, even, just. It also stands for balance and equilibrium. What do these words mean to you and how do they relate to this book?

Equilibrium is described as a state in which opposing forces and influences are balanced. In this book we have discussed these forces already many times. We have spoken about the Tiger and the Dragon, the hard and soft, the fast and slow, the left and right, the conscious and the unconscious, the scholar and the warrior, and now.. Here is another.

The Chinese philosophy concept of Yin and Yang and how all opposite and contrary forces are interconnected.

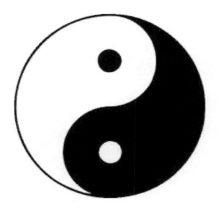

You see, there cannot be one without the other. Good and bad cannot exist if not for the other. There are many natural examples of these dualities. We can see it in light and dark, hot and cold, life and death. All of these are actually complimentary forces interacting to form a dynamic system in which *the whole is greater than the parts*.

There is a natural ebb and flow to the universe, a natural harmonisation of life and it can be seen in the ocean, in the motion of waves - in the push and pull. In electricity, we see the same phenomenon - the return and the current. Everything has a hard and a soft, a positive and a negative balance.

With the Yin Yang symbol, Yin represents the dark shady side of the mountain, the North slope in the shade of Yang, the sunny south slope. Yin is soft and yielding, associated with water, night and femininity. Yang is hard, fast, solid and focused, associated with fire, the sun and masculinity.

So, how is this relative to us? How can we use this knowledge to our advantage? How can we learn from the great masters, so that we too can be inspired to greatness?

In martial arts, in my Kenpo class, we learn principles such as, *'Go with the path of least resistance.'*

We learn to go with it rather than pull against it. We learn to use the strength of others to our advantage; we learn to see that strength as a good thing and how to make the most of it. **How can you use the strength of others to your advantage?**

- **Think about this now and write down your thought…..**
  Think about the people you know, what strengths they have and what can you gain and learn from these strengths?

You see with any emotional balance, all acting influences are cancelled out by others thus resulting in a stable, balanced system.

Going with the path of least resistance, leads me to another key principle that we learn, **Economy of Motion**.

- *How does this translate for you?*

- *How can you work smarter, not harder?*

To achieve your goals it is often wise to ask for help. Learn from all the great experts. They do what they know best and always ask for help. They know that this makes sense. So as to maximise their own time productively they value their time and their skills. They know what they are good at and what they are not good at and they go and find people who can help them with the latter. Look at who are your experts, who are you surrounded by, who can help you. Build your team! Weigh up all your valuable time and take note, what you have been wasting it on.

Write down now, *3 things that you have been wasting time on, up to now- that you could either give up, delegate, or ask someone more knowledgeable on the subject to help you with.*

_____

_____

_____

Decide to take action today on at least one of the above!

In other words, ask for help, you will be surprised at how many people will gladly oblige. Find easier ways;

Take the path of least resistance.

Do the same with your brain. Sometimes the answer is the one staring us in the face. It is the most obvious. The one we didn't see at first. We have our blinkers on again. Use your super brain to find the answer. Access your best state with your exercises. Practice your Qi Gong, Meditate and *Sleep on it!*

Yes, exactly like we are told to do sometimes. Sleep on it. Your brain will process all the information you need during the night and in the morning the answer will be clearer. Trust your unconscious; it is always working hard for you.

If you can't think of the answer, Say out loud; *'The answer will come to me in a minute'*... and it will ☺

Have you ever said, *'it's on the tip of my tongue'*, and then a short while later, you suddenly remember? That's because your unconscious was still searching for you, still working hard, even when you and your conscious mind had stopped searching. Your unconscious keeps doing its job, just for you, busily looking until it finds the information you had required.

As I have said already, there is a hard and soft to everything. We have another principle in our martial arts.....

109

Every block is a strike

In other words everything we do for self-defence is also making us stronger for our attack and stepping us a little closer to conquering our goal. Every time you take care of an aspect of your health, mental, physical or spiritual, you are building your resources and your strengths. You are protecting yourself but you are also building your strength armour for your final attack on your goal.

We often think change has to be slow, when in fact change is very fast, in fact it happens in an instant. But before the moment of change, there was all the preparation that led up to that moment. That's what practice does.

So, practice physically and practice mentally. When you visualize (*you know now to do it with emotion*), use your actual limbs as much as possible. Like a golfer practices his swing, like a martial artist who imitates his masters moves. Do the moves in your head just make sure you have INTENT!

Any micro-muscle movements that your brain detects will be stored in your unconscious. This is how muscle memory works. This is how to teach martial arts, a sport or in fact anything that you want to reappear 'spontaneously' in the future. In fact practicing in your head is even better than practicing for real, because this way you can do it each time perfectly! Exactly how you want it to turn out and as you know, your unconscious will think you're an absolute expert!

We also talk in martial arts terms about **Marriage of Gravity**. We use the gravitational force and our body weight to add more force or power. Gravitational force could be considered as bringing your weight to bear in a technique. The same principle can be used in life, if you bring your weight to bear, ie; the sum of your conscious and your subconscious, you will have explosive results. When you synchronise it all together, then you start to understand how to harness the natural balance to create huge momentum.

Bruce Lee was famous for his One Inch Punch, an incredibly powerful and explosive strike that he was able to generate from a very close distance. He was able to do this by using back up mass, with synergy of his Chi, all of his energy.

Imagine this back up mass is the sum of everything you know and contain.
When you concentrate all your energy and focus on moving it to one spot it can be transformational.
Think of a writer and the tip of the pen is the conduit by which he releases his potential.

Bruce Lee was also well known for his incredible balance and ability to use his centre of gravity and his core very wisely. If you are unbalanced, out of kilter, if your centre is off, in a martial sense you are exposed. Your centre line is open to attack - so too in life. You can achieve this equilibrium by synchronising your external goals with internal peace. By practicing your breathing, Qi Gong, visualisation and a balance in life, you are well on your way to achieving this.

I spoke at the start of this chapter about equal meaning 'the same as'. It is wise for us to always remember that, no matter how high we soar, we can always fall back down and someday... we will.

You see.. we are all in the same circle of life.

Remember your purpose, for it will give you **tenacity**.

Put out goodness into the world;
Be of service to your fellow man,
Without any thought of return,
and the universe will balance the book of life for you.

Now, write down now,
3 things you can do to help others this week;

_____

_____

_____

_____

Do not do good to get something out of it
but rather to put into the ether of life.

Set your compass to true North.

In Kenpo we are taught to keep our head level. In Infinite Insights Volume 1, Ed Parker (*Founder of American Kenpo*) speaks of your head being like a ships gyro.

'A gyro remains unaffected by the pitching and rolling movement of a ship. No matter how rough the water or what position a ship may be forced into, the gyro remains parallel with the horizon'

....and enables the captain to steer a true course.

What is your true course?
Write out now how you can help others and contribute to this world.

Write what is your mission – your voyage.

_____

_____

_____

_____

_____

We use the word 'level' in many ways. We say things such as level-headed, levelling things out, a level playing field, on the level. So these metaphors are inherent in our mind-set already, we just have to bring them to the fore to give ourselves a sense of equilibrium. Now, to truly get that sense of equilibrium, I suggest 2 things.

(1) – Dream really BIG. Go *wild*!

As though nothing can stop you and you are already there.
Justin Tranz says 'Dare to Fail!'

***'Shoot for the stars
and you will land on the moon.'***

(2) - Plan for failure!
......*Screech!...What?? I can hear you doing a double take!*

What I really mean is...**plan for the obstacles**. ☺
Plan now what you will do when you encounter adversity and any hurdles you need to overcome, so that, you don't just quit at the first hurdle or first sign of trouble. This way you have planned for it all and are ready to fight.

The TRUE Path to Success, you see is NOT like this....

But is actually like this >....

So, plan for adversity now!

Write down 5 what if's....
*5 things that may happen on my way to achieving
my goal and how I will overcome them.*

_____

_____

_____

_____

_____

Being balanced means being sensibly crazy!

Planning your strategy, step by step makes perfect sense. You don't have to see the whole staircase, just the 1st step.....except.... I am actually going to take you backwards!

What??

Remember what I said about motivation coming first and your mind not knowing the difference between what's real and imagined? Okay great, so here is how this works.

You decide your dream goal. Dream BIG now. Then we imagine it and create it, so our unconscious thinks you have been there already. Then we go backwards. Yes! And we look at how we got there – a lot less daunting then going forward, so let's do it!

I call this Exercise....
'From Tiger to Dragon and back again'....* [7]

- Get comfortable because you are going for the trip of your life time. Into your future!
- Close your eyes and breathe deep.
- Take mental note of where you are in your seat, so you know where to come back to ☺

---

[7] * Based on the work of Dr. Richard Bandler

- Imagine yourself floating up and out of your body, looking down on yourself at this present moment.
- Float up and look forward, imagining your future ahead of you, stretching out in a beautiful gold shimmering line.
- Look at the near horizon and where the goal you want to achieve is.
- Keep in mind where the present you is, as you slowly start to drift forward in time, towards this point, looking down on your timeline and your life as you pass it by.
- Bring yourself up to the point in time when you have achieved this goal. Look down and move closer to have a good look. See how happy the future you is having achieved the desired goal. Watch how you move, behave, act and speak. See what you are doing and how you are feeling. Take a good long look and enjoy it.
- Now, this is the most important bit. Very slowly, float back towards the present, stopping at each moment in time to see what steps you took to get you to your desired goal. Look very carefully and take note of what you did.
- When you have learnt from all the experiences and took all this information with you, float back to where you sit in the present moment and allow yourself to float back into your body.

- Keep your eyes closed for as long as you need, while you allow all this information to be fully absorbed. Remember the experience you had in your future, knowing that now you have been there it will now be much easier as you know clearly all the steps you have to take.

****

Remember, if you can dream it in your internal world,
then you can make it a reality in your external world.
Once you have experienced the elation of manifesting it in your
imagination, your mind will move mountains
to make it a reality.

Experience has proven that if we have something taken away from us,
we will fight much harder to get it back,
more so than if we never had it in the first place.
This is what our intentional dreams will do for us.
Dream with intent, go there and experience all that you desire and allow
your unconscious to do the rest.

NB: As another special bonus go to www.theblackbeltmastermind.com/bonuses to download your special recording of me talking you through this wonderful experience! Pssst.....Password MASTER ☺

CHAPTER 7 -

Brown responsibility –
The wisdom of Results

'The only limitations one has,
is the one he places upon himself.'
Muhammad Ali

We are all, in the jungle of life. We survive as best we can - we hunt and gather for sustenance, we watch out for predators and protect our young. We all begin as the tiger does, moving stealthily and warily amongst the trees and obstacles before us.

But the dragon, instead, lives above the trees. He looks down from a higher view point. He can see things from a whole new angle, a new perspective. He has stepped out of his box, transformed from a tiger into a dragon, merged his colours and his stripes together, grown wings and flown upwards - for he has attained wisdom.

This is the ultimate goal in martial arts, to reach this stage of enlightenment, to become the dragon. In life, we strive for the same. We strive for this wisdom so that we can master the art of conquering life to the fullest.

As a tiger you knew how to react. The dragon stage you are now entering, will also teach you how to 'act', or what we call pre-emptive action. We can take this here to mean *to create so as to obtain and get results*!

For transformational change to happen you need to set goals. Create your goals. The process is simple. We start with an idea.

Look around you. ***Everything you see started at some point with the seed of an idea.***

The next step is to transform this idea into reality.

First thing to always keep in mind is, if you truly want change to happen, then things can and will change.

Even without actively changing the situation, everything evolves, all is temporary. We know this from experience and from the previous chapter on the natural balance of life. But we can help things along if we so wish. Keep referring to what you have learnt so far. Remember the voice in your head, stay **Aware** of what you say to yourself.

Take negative words such as "stuck," "ruined," and "defeated" out of your vocabulary. Instead fill your mind with inspiring and motivating words such as "just", "nearly" and "about to", these are much more productive to getting you to your destination and signify a nearing to reaching your goal.

The word "Try" is also one to never use again as when you use this; you are implying failure to your unconscious. Instead of 'I will try to ....' replace it with 'I will do...'. This is much more convincing to you consciously and unconsciously!

As the saying by Henry Ford goes,
'Whether you think you can,
or you think you can't,
you're right.'

Okay, so you have an idea now what?

Many people have hundreds of ideas a day, sometimes good ones, occasionally spectacular. But many do nothing with these ideas.

They think them up but still carry on sitting in front of the television, munching on their Mars bar and complaining how their life is mundane, boring, difficult or impossible.

The next thing is they see the same idea they had thought of on the TV screen and hear a story of how this person changed their life with this simple thought.

Then they complain about how it was typical luck, how it was easier for that person, how it is harder for them because…bla bla, and the cycle starts all over again.

Now I understand this perfectly, for believe me, I have done this myself a lot in the past and I know how enticing and addictive this way of thinking is. My life changed though the day I decided to stop being a victim and take **response-ability**.

We have covered this of course in previous chapters and you are by now aware of how to change that limiting belief and those bad habitual thoughts. You have the ability to ask artful, smarter questions, so as to get you thinking in a more fruitful way and you also know how to build up the **Tenacity** to get you there.

What we are going to do now is learn from the wisdom of the Dragon, so you too can look down and see the wood from the trees. We will look at your goals from another perspective….. that of the Dragon.

Exercise - 'Looking through the Dragon's eye'...* [8]

- Get comfortable, take a couple of deep breaths and relax.
- Imagine someone in front of you that you admire greatly for their wisdom. This can be a loved family member like your Grandfather, a famous person like Ghandi, a fictional person like Obi-Wan Kenobi, from Star Trek, or even a beautiful and wise Dragon, as long as you see them as a font of wisdom.
- Look at this character who is watching you and imagine you are the greatest of friends. This character has as much admiration for you as you do for them. Tell them about your idea or the goals you want to achieve.
- Now, imagine yourself floating up out of your body and into theirs.
- Look at yourself sitting in this chair and see it from their perspective, from their eyes of love and respect.
- Imagine now being as them, how you now feel. What do you think looking at the '*you*' in the chair. What do you say to that other you. What advice and words of wisdom do you give, from this place of knowledge, experience and a new perspective.

---

[8] * Based on the work of Dr.Richard Bandler

- Take all the time you need, as you explore this new mind-set and attitude you are now living in. Look at your idea or goal from this point of wisdom and take all that you need to learn from it.
- Now, speak these words to the 'you' in the chair. Tell that *'you'* what they need to do to achieve their dream. Tell them with all the love, passion and belief that you have inside from this place of knowledge.
- When you have passed on all that you need to, float back into your body and allow this new information to absorb.
- Enjoy this new perspective and get up and take action!

Now that you can see things through the Dragons eyes, use this time to write down from this new perspective, the top 5 steps you can take from now, to get you towards your goal or help your idea to become reality.

You know that if you do nothing,
you will get nothing,
SO...
It is time now,

to take **massive** *action!*

5 Steps I can take to make my idea a reality!

_____

_____

_____

_____

So now that you have some clear steps that you will take, let's reinforce your tenacity by making sure you are in the very best possible state. We have concentrated throughout this book on your mind-set, which is what this book is about, but let's just briefly cover some other aspects. I believe that they are all interconnected. As well as your mental state we have your physical and spiritual state. How have you planned to take care and nurture these also?

I am not going to write a treatise on all these various elements, as that is for a whole other book! But I will outline some good points of interest. Now is a good time for you to look at each of these areas and see how you can improve on them.

We have covered our mental and spiritual side to an extent in previous chapters and we discussed how surrounding yourself with the right people will help you. We learnt that **_what you feast your mind on will become your reality,_** so feast it on good stuff!

We mentioned meditation, visualisation and constantly striving to improve yourself and others.

Challenge will help you grow, so challenge yourself to do something new every day. Go out meet people, love with a passion and share your message. Watch funny films, comedy shows, laugh, hug and kiss lots, as it floods your body with dopamine and serotonin, the feel-good chemicals of your brain. ☺

*Learn something new every day
and your world will open up.*

Write down now 3 things you will start to do today, to open your world up and broaden your horizon.

_____

_____

_____

Now have a look at the physical side of things. What can you do to improve this and why bother? Well, you know they are interconnected right? If you feel lethargic physically it will affect your mental state, exactly the same as feeling tired mentally will affect your physical state. Often we say such things as 'oh, I am too tired to exercise.' But, you do know that exercising will help you feel less tired, don't you?

Well if you didn't, you do now. Exercising will help you feel better in so many ways. You will feel more alert and invigorated and be able to focus and work much more productively. A simple 30 minute brisk walk, in the fresh air will increase your productivity about 30%. I mentioned fresh air because another aspect I am adamant about is getting daylight every day.

Keep away from too many electrical positive Ions; get out into the wilderness and away from all the computers. It is crucial to helping you feel good. Again it is recommended that you get 30 minutes standard day light every day so that you get your Vitamin D and don't suffer from SAD. (Seasonal Affective Disorder). Of course, do remember your sun protection also!

Write down now;
3 ways I can improve on my daily fresh air and exercise routine.

_____

_____

_____

Talking about daylight, leads me to the opposite - night time and your sleep.

Of course you know that this is another major factor with your mood, concentration and productivity. It is vital that you get a good night's sleep. Some suggestions I would make are-

- Sleep in a warm but well ventilated room.
- Switch off all electrical equipment and keep as far away as possible.
- Wind down before you sleep. Take a relaxing lavender bath, drink a cup of camomile tea or listen to some relaxing classical music.
- When you sleep you go through a 90 minute cycle. It is best to wake up after one of these, not during, or you will feel very groggy, as you have woke during the deepest part of sleep, the RIM part (Rapid Eye Movement). Set your sleep time for either 4 ½, 6, 7 ½ or 9 hours. You will feel much more alert.
- Wake up naturally as much as possible
(*more on that in a minute!*)
- Use a Sunlight alarm to wake you, this is much more natural for your system especially if you happen to have to rise in the dark.
Often, these have birds chirping or nice soft music; just get something better than the horrible screeching sound of most alarms!
Not a great way to start your day!

Write down now;

1 way which I can immediately improve my sleeping routine.

Another hugely important aspect is of course your diet. This alone could fill volumes and although I am not a qualified Nutritionist I am very well versed and interested in the subject!

So, I will simply touch on foods that I love and that I know are particularly good for your brain and your productivity.

The rule of thumb is basically to eat foods that resemble food, ie; not processed food. Eat bright, coloured natural foods. Fill your shopping trolley with LOTS of fruit and vegetables.

Add colour to your plate and add colour to your life.

Drink more water, eat less sugar and refined foods and cut down on caffeine and alcohol.

**My top foods for your brain and your mood
are as follows;**

Lots of nuts and seeds –
(Walnuts, Almonds, Cashews, Sesame seeds, etcetera.)
Full of Vitamin E and Omega 3's, which helps against
Cognitive decline, plus they hugely increase our Melatonin
level, which is a sleep regulating hormone.
(Grate or soak them if you find them hard on your digestion)

Avocados –
Again High in Omega 3's, helping you to have healthy blood
flow and a healthy brain. They are also said to lower blood
pressure.

Wheat germ –
Again high in Omega's and Vitamin E.
Sprinkle on your cereal or in soups.

Berries –
Full of antioxidants which help protect the brain from
oxidative stress. Plus they significantly improve both learning
capacity and motor neuron skills and help reduce depression.

Green Vegetables-
Full of antioxidants again, Iron and Zinc. Both good for
energy and your brain. Full of Photo-nutrients which help
protect you against viruses.

Spinach-
Full of Vitamin C, E and Iron, and known to increase
Dopamine, the pleasure chemical.

Coloured foods such as, Carrots, tomatoes and oranges
Contain a high level of Lutein, which reduces age related
memory loss and inflammation of the brain.
Also helps eye sight.

Garlic –
Stimulates the production of chemicals that help cells
withstand stress. Also is a natural antiseptic and great for
your blood.

Turmeric-
Antioxidant and anti-inflammatory.
Helps against Alzheimer's and protects against cancer.

Rosemary –
Stimulates the Pineal Gland and improves energy levels.

Sage –
A good memory enhancer.

I could of course go on and on, this is just to give you the general idea ☺

Write down; 3 ways I will improve my diet today!

_____

_____

_____

Okay so, now that we have a much more productive plan for how to get the results we desire, let's talk about your clock. Remember, I said previously I would talk about how to wake up naturally? Well, what I meant by that was yes, we can. We actually very rarely need an alarm clock. This is because; we all contain an internal clock. Our conscious may sleep, but our unconscious keeps our internal time clock ticking constantly. Tick tock, tick tock.....

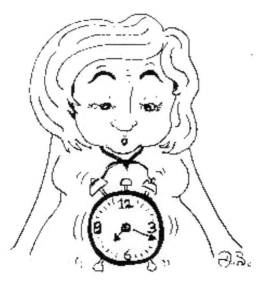

Many people have experienced this by stating they wanted to wake up at a certain time, going to sleep and then waking up a moment before the alarm. It happens for me most days!

I simply set my internal clock. You can too.

Tonight before bed, decide what time you want to awaken and then visualise this time in your mind's eye. Tell your unconscious to wake you at this time and then go to sleep. My bet is you will awaken just before your alarm!

This is because of our internal clock. Our unconscious keeps working even when we sleep. Of course it does, if not we would be dead! ☺

If you don't believe me by now, think about when you are fast asleep and you wake up suddenly because of a loud noise. Who woke you?? It was your unconscious of course! In the same way, when you drive home and can't remember how you got there. Who drove? Your unconscious of course!

Another example? Think of a time you were 'switched off', driving again in another world (*your conscious brain was resting*), and suddenly you come back into full alertness because of a cat running out in front of the car. Who alerted you? Your unconscious of course, once again. This is what happens when in hypnosis or trance. Many people believe they are not in control, when in fact, of course they are.

You are simply going into a deep, relaxed state just like when you are absorbed in a film or a specific task.

Your conscious mind has switched off but your unconscious is always there to alert you of any danger or uncomfortable situation you may want to remove yourself from.

You are always in control when in a trance. Your unconscious will protect you. So trance away, happily in the knowledge you have a loving protector watching over you.

This leads me to the last of our lovely exercises and another martial arts principle (*developed by Ed Parker*).

The Clock Principle.

Imagine you are standing in the centre of a clock which is underneath you. Directly in front of you is 12 o'clock, behind you 6pm, to your right 3 pm, to your left 9pm. It is based on a method called referencing and helps us always know where we are.

We can use this also in life, so that at any particular point in our lives we know where we are and where we are going- because we use the clock principle. Most of us view our lives and our timeline as a straight line vertically in front of us, or else we view it as moving horizontally in front of us. Both ways can be very useful in different aspects.

With the clock principle, like that of a watch or a clock, you can have present time or ....wait for it.... you can turn the hands back or project forward. Controlling any particular time you wish. Just like a time machine!

Have you ever wanted to go back and change the past? Or wished you had appreciated a certain moment more? How does all this benefit us getting the results we want?

Just like when we experienced a different viewpoint so as to gain more knowledge, we can also gain more knowledge from learning new unexplored insights from the past.

You can also go forward. You can imagine something you want to take place at a certain time, make it specific! Set your internal clock. Tell it to remind you at regular intervals and give you a final alarm call on such a date you have specified. Watch and see how this pops into your mind at exactly the times you specified!

When you go back in time, if you so wish, you can then also reconstruct events. Because you are in control of your mind clock!

Let's have a look at both right now, with this time machine of yours!

We're going back to the future!

Exercise –
Your Mind Clock- Tick tock, tick tock....* [9]

- Look at the time and notice the hands where they point.

- Now get comfortable, close your eyes, take a few deep breaths and hold on tight!
- Imagine yourself standing in the centre of a beautiful, giant clock, facing 12 o clock. This is your mind clock make it really special. Notice the hands pointing to whatever time you saw before you closed your eyes.
- Now, imagine yourself, crouching down and starting to pull the big hand backwards, causing the small hand to move accordingly with it.
- Allow the hands to build momentum as you stand in the centre spot, watching them spin.
- Let your unconscious guide you back to a time that you would like to examine more in-depth and learn from.
  A time when you achieved results; an occasion that you excelled in or an event that you felt proud of.
- Trust your unconscious to bring the hands to a stop when the time is right.

---

[9] * Based on the work of Dr. Richard Bandler

- Once here, now watch where you are and look at what you notice, as a detached, time traveller. Notice the things you never seen before and take what you need from this experience. Learn from what this other you did.
- Now slowly start the hands spinning forward again, and watch your past life as it flashes by you in slow motion.
- Stop it anytime you want to examine in more detail, something that can help you. Take particular note of all the experience and knowledge that you have accumulated over the years. Pick up these inner resources and bring them with you, knowing you possessed them all along.
- Arrive back at the present time and allow the hands to settle as you also absorb all the realisation of all the things that you have done and achieved in your life so far.
- Take your time, before you open your eyes in the present time, knowing you have so many experiences and resources that will now help you to achieve your goals!

Sometimes life can only be understood backwards.
Our past teaches us, while our future is our creation.
This moment is our choice and our gift,
which is why it is called the Present...

CHAPTER 8

Black - Mystery and Protection

Achieving your Black belt...
The end...or is it?

So you are here now. You have arrived at the Dragon stage it appears, but first, have a good peek into the Dragons eyes, look through the black and see what you see. Yes, those specks of white.

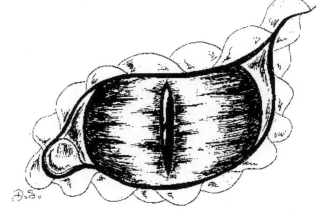

For what do they represent exactly if not going back to the beginning, back to your white belt. For we know that we never stop evolving, because as already said, repetition is the mother of perfection.

Are you disappointed by this? Of course you're not! Otherwise you would have not learnt anything yet.

You know full well that 'ignorance is bliss' but being aware of your ignorance is the first step towards enlightenment. I know this is a path you dearly want to continue on, for it is addictive. Once we realise the pleasure to be gleaned from being aware of our evolvement, we always want to continue on learning.

Be aware of the one who thinks he knows it ALL for he is the most ignorant

Life itself and your improvement is a continuous cycle. We never stop learning and we never stop evolving. It is a circle with no beginning and no end. In life we can see these patterns and structures, such as the circle and other geometrical archetypes everywhere. We can see them in nature, in a miniscule particle of sand or a beautiful snow flake and we can also see expressions of life in more visible examples, such as in movement.

All of them follow the same geometrical pattern, outlining the metaphysical principle of our inseparable relationship, to the parts as a whole.

In martial arts this movement is represented by the **'Universal Pattern'** created by Ed Parker. Often misunderstood as a flat two dimensional illustration. Instead, I want you to envisage yourself standing in the middle of one of these spheres now. You are in the centre of this Universal Pattern which is repeating itself over and over on every axil. It is three dimensional!

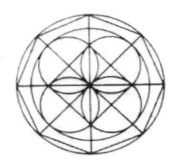

See it clearly from this perspective, as multi-dimensional and you have a lot more freedom in your movement, as you have in life. We talk about the circle, the triangle, the diamond, the straight line, and the figure eight, all overlapping and encompassed in this sphere.

This is the ultimate expression of unity, completeness and everlasting movement. It represents motion at its most complete.

Always remember from now on, to use your 'lateral' thinking cap, when looking at problems. Look at them three dimensionally. Step outside of them as you have learnt to do and look at them from another perspective. Look at working through adversity and obstacles from new angles, challenge the thoughts you have and keep asking more useful questions. Tackle tasks in a new way and from a new path.

**Think multi dimensionally and
you will start to see your world in a new way.**

Today is a new day. ***Carpe Diem!***

See all the abundance and opportunities before you that will move your life in the direction you want it to go. Keep the momentum going as with that circle.

Remember that 'I've got your back', I have after all got to know you now, I have travelled this far with you and I am eager to see where this next exciting part of your road takes you. I would love to hear from you! Come chat to me at www.theblackbeltmastermind.com

Most of all enjoy the journey, enjoy the learning, and keep going just like in the circle of life, because after all, as you already know…

A black belt is simply..
a white belt, who never gave up.

RESOURCES & FURTHER READING

This is a brief but by no means comprehensive list of some further reading that I have loved and that I would recommend if you are interested in NLP, the mind, your spiritual development or any further personal development.

'Make Your Life Great', Guide to Trance – Formation by Richard Bandler

'Change Your Life in Seven Days', by Paul McKenna

'You Can Have What You Want', by Michael Neill

'The Charismatic Edge', by Owen Fitzpatrick

'Thinking, Fast and Slow', by Daniel Kahneman

'The Alchemist', by Paolo Coelho

'A Return to Love', by Marianne Williamson

''The First Phone Call from Heaven', by Mitch Album

'Jonathan Livingston Seagull', by Richard Bach

'The Power of Now', by Eckhart Tolle

'Man's Search for Meaning', by Viktor Frankl

ABOUT THE AUTHOR....

Danielle Serpico is a qualified Master Neuro-Linguistic Practitioner (NLP) and Trainer with the Society of NLP. She has trained directly with Dr. Richard Bandler himself (co-founder of NLP), as well as many other renown hypnosis experts, such as Paul McKenna, Owen Fitzpatrick and Justin Tranz.

A martial artist, self defence consultant and European champion, Danielle has trained with a host of renowned experts, most notably Tommy Jordan 10th Degree Grand Master, Kenpo Karate IKA, Erle Montaigue, Masters Degree China and Founder of The World Taiji Boxing Association and Grand Master Larry Tatum, Ed Parkers American Kenpo. Danielle certainly knows how to help you protect yourself, not only physically but mentally as well.

With an entrepreneurial background, 20 years' experience running her own business, managing large staff, motivating and coaching others, Danielle is the one to have in your corner.

She runs regular workshops and motivational seminars as well as private consultations. In her spare time her other passion is to paint colourful inspirations on large canvases, as well as writing her self-help books, children's books and her fantasy fiction novel. She presently lives by the sea in Wicklow, the garden of Ireland.

For more information, resources and details of upcoming seminars and workshops - visit
www.theblackbeltmastermind.com

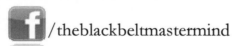 /theblackbeltmastermind

 @DanielleSerpico

 danielleserpico

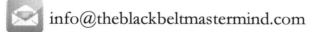 info@theblackbeltmastermind.com

NB: Remember go get your FREE Bonuses at
www.theblackbeltmastermind.com/bonuses
with your secret password ;-) *Enjoy the journey!!!*

Printed in Great Britain
by Amazon